FUZZY LOGIC BASED IN OPTIMIZATION METHODS AND CONTROL SYSTEMS AND ITS APPLICATIONS

Edited by **Ali Sadollah**

Fuzzy Logic Based in Optimization Methods and Control Systems and Its Applications
http://dx.doi.org/10.5772/intechopen.73112
Edited by Ali Sadollah

Contributors

Abdelwaheb Aydi, M Venkateshkumar, Anoop Sathyan, Kelly Cohen, Bloul Benattia, Anjali Munde, Ali Sadollah

Notice

Statements and opinions expressed in the chapters are these of the individual contributors and not necessarily those of the editors or publisher. No responsibility is accepted for the accuracy of information contained in the published chapters. The publisher assumes no responsibility for any damage or injury to persons or property arising out of the use of any materials, instructions, methods or ideas contained in the book.

First published in London, United Kingdom, 2018 by IntechOpen

IntechOpen is the global imprint of INTECHOPEN LIMITED, registered in England and Wales, registration number: 11086078, The Shard, 25th floor, 32 London Bridge Street
London, SE19SG – United Kingdom
Printed in Croatia

British Library Cataloguing-in-Publication Data
A catalogue record for this book is available from the British Library

Additional hard copies can be obtained from orders@intechopen.com

Fuzzy Logic Based in Optimization Methods and Control Systems and Its Applications, Edited by Ali Sadollah
p. cm.
Print ISBN 978-1-78984-067-4
Online ISBN 978-1-78984-068-1

Meet the editor

Ali Sadollah received his BS degree in Mechanical Engineering from University Azad Semnan, Iran, in 2007 and his MS degree in Mechanical Engineering from the University of Semnan, Semnan, Iran, in 2010. He obtained his PhD at the Faculty of Engineering, University of Malaya, Kuala Lumpur, Malaysia, in 2013. Also, he was a postdoctoral research fellow for more than 2 years at Korea University, Seoul, South Korea. In 2016, for a year he was a member of the research staff at Nanyang Technological University, Singapore. Currently, he is guest assistant professor at Sharif University of Technology. His research interests include algorithm development, metaheuristics, applications of soft computing methods in engineering, artificial neural networks, fuzzy logic and its applications, etc.

Contents

Preface

In recent years, the number and variety of applications of fuzzy logic have increased considerably. Applications range from consumer products such as cameras, camcorders, washing machines, and microwave ovens to industrial process control, medical instrumentation, decision-support systems, portfolio selection, among others.

In this book, the theory and applications of fuzzy logic are highlighted by describing different aspects of fuzzy logic. The book starts with a simple but fundamental question and then evolutionary optimization methods are used to fine tune fuzzy logic parameters. The book ends with some practical research on the application of fuzzy logic to various fields of study from energy efficiency to solid waste landfill management.

I would like to thank all the authors and scholars for their precious contributions to this book. Special thanks go to IntechOpen and Author Service Manager Mrs. Marina Dusevic for their support and patience.

Ali Sadollah
Sharif University of Technology
Tehran, Iran

Theory of Fuzzy Logic

Chapter 1

Introductory Chapter: Which Membership Function is Appropriate in Fuzzy System?

Ali Sadollah

Additional information is available at the end of the chapter

http://dx.doi.org/10.5772/intechopen.79552

1. Role of membership functions

Fuzzy logic systems are widely used for control, system identification, pattern recognition problems, and many more applications from industry to academia. The membership functions (MFs) play vital role in the overall performance of fuzzy representation. The MFs are the building blocks of fuzzy set theory, that is, fuzziness in a fuzzy set is determined by its MF. Accordingly, the shapes of MFs are important for a particular problem since they effect on a fuzzy inference system. They may have different shapes such as triangular, trapezoidal, Gaussian, and so forth. The only condition a MF must really satisfy is that it must vary between 0 and 1.

2. How to choose an appropriate membership function?

The MFs can be of any shape and form as long as it maps the given data with desirable degree of memberships. As far as choice of MFs is concerned, it is us to decide. This is where fuzzy system offers individual degrees of freedom. With experience, one will come to know which shape of MF is good for the application under consideration.

As there are infinite number of ways to characterize fuzziness, there are infinite number of ways to graphically depict the MFs that describe this fuzziness. The choice of which of the methods to use depends entirely on the problem size and problem type. Instead of choosing the shape of MF, setting the interval and number of MFs are also very important. For instance, to model a temperature control system by fuzzy logic, it is really important to know how many MFs are needed (e.g., low, med, and high MF) and also choosing the intervals of MFs. These two factors also have a great impact on the outcome of a fuzzy logic system.

In addition, looking at the distribution of the data is a good idea. Although, trial and error method is often used for MF shape, because there is no exact method for choosing the MFs. The shape of MFs depends on how one believes in a given linguistic variable. It is more a question of intuition then criteria. The only condition a MF must really satisfy is that it must vary between 0 and 1. The function itself can be an arbitrary curve whose shape we can define as a function that suits us from the point of view of simplicity, convenience, speed, and efficiency. Therefore, the type of MF doesnot play a crucial role in shaping how the model performs.

However, the number of MF has greater influence as it determines the computational time. Hence, the optimum model can be determined by varying the number/type of MFs for achieving best system performance. Ref. [1] discusses which shape is best if one uses fuzzy logic as a universal approximator. Also, a constrained interpolations scheme was developed for fitting a MF to a finite number of known membership values [2].

There are many references giving directions of how to choose MF [3–6]. The basic problem with modeling a situation, is to break the 0–1 modeling. This can be done by using triangular MF. However, if the situation is complex and deep, we might need a special type of MF. For instance, if the problem at hand is a quantum mechanics problem, then a special MF is needed. In order to make the best choice, one needs a lot of "experience" with the given situation. This experience will tune up and best fit, the subjective choice of the researcher with the given reality. There is no objective way to do so. Thus, a high fidelity intuition based on sufficient experience will give an acceptable answer.

Generally speaking, triangular MF is one of the most encountered MF in practice. Of highly applied MFs, the triangular MFs are formed using straight lines. These straight line membership functions have the advantage of simplicity. Gaussian MFs are popular methods for specifying fuzzy sets because of their smoothness and concise notation. These curves have the advantage of being smooth and nonzero at all points.

It is advisable to use the symmetric triangular MF with 50% overlap, and then apply tuning procedure during which we can either change the left and/or right spread and/or overlapping. This is to be continued till we get satisfactory results. Same approach can be attempted for other shapes such as trapezoidal, bell-shape, and so forth.

Triangular shapes represent fuzzy numbers, while trapezoid shapes represent fuzzy intervals. These are the simplest shapes. Other different shapes can be obtained from transformations of the triangle induced by linguistic modifiers, truth-functional modifiers, compositions, projections, and other operations.

In fact, the selection of MF shape is problem specific. Based on extensive review on many literatures, it can be concluded that the triangular MF is widely used because of its simplicity. Using various MF for given problems, usually Gaussian and triangular MFs are found to be closely performing well and better than other types of MF. In specific, the triangular MF is found to be better than Gaussian MF. Zhao and Bose [7] compared the response of the system with various MFs and conveyed that the triangular MF is superior to any other MFs.

Indeed, if one has no priority on the shape of MFs, triangular or trapezoidal shapes are simple to implement and fast for computation. However, if one has some priorities on their shapes (e.g., from histograms on sampled data), it may be interested to build MFs with shapes derived from these a priori shapes after some smoothing if needed.

Afterwards, the question is what the optimal values of initial parameters are that we need to be aware of to make a sensible choice of the chosen MF?

In order to maximize their performance, it is often necessary to undertake a design optimization process in which the adjustable parameters defining a particular fuzzy system are tuned to maximize a given performance criterion. Using metaheuristic optimization methods and evolutionary optimization algorithms, fuzzy logic possesses the great flexibility toward its initial parameters regarding MFs [8].

Interested reader can find some useful information about MFs and some procedures (e.g., GA and neural network) to assign memberships to fuzzy variables [4]. There are many articles, which have used optimization algorithms such as particle swarm optimization and genetic algorithm to find the optimal set of parameters for fuzzy models [9–12].

Author details

Ali Sadollah

Address all correspondence to: ali_sadollah@yahoo.com

School of Mechanical Engineering, Sharif University of Technology, Tehran, Iran

References

[1] Kosko B, Mitaim S. What is the best shape for a fuzzy set in function approximation? Proceedings of the 5th IEEE International Conference on Fuzzy Systems (FUZZ-96); September 1996. pp. 1237-1243

[2] Chen JE, Otto KN. Constructing membership functions using interpolation and measurement theory. Fuzzy Sets and Systems. 1995;**73**(3):313-327

[3] Wu D. Twelve considerations in choosing between Gaussian and trapezoidal membership functions in interval type-2 fuzzy logic controllers. IEEE International Conference on Fuzzy Systems (FUZZ-IEEE); 2012; Brisbane, QLD, Australia

[4] Ross TJ. Fuzzy Logic with Engineering Applications. 3ed. John Wiley & Sons; 2010

[5] Rutkowska A. Influence of membership function's shape on portfolio optimization results. 2016;**6** (1):45-54

[6] Czekalski P. Evolution-fuzzy rule based system with parameterized consequences. International Journal of Applied Mathematics and Computer Science. 2006;**16**(3):373-385

[7]   Zhao J, Bose BK. Evaluation of membership functions for fuzzy logic controlled induction motor drive. 28th Annual IEEE Conference of the Industrial Electronics Society 2002; Sevilla; Spain

[8]   El-Zonkoly AM, Khalil AA, Ahmied NM. Optimal tuning of lead-lag and fuzzy logic power system stabilizers using particle swarm optimization. Expert Systems with Applications. 2009;**36**(2):2097-2106

[9]   Zhang W, Liu Y. Fuzzy logic controlled particle swarm for reactive power optimization considering voltage stability. IEEE International Conference on Power Engineering, Singapore. 2005;**2005**:1-5

[10] Esmin AAA, Aoki AR, Lambert-Torres G. Particle swarm optimization for fuzzy membership functions optimization. In: IEEE International Conference on Systems, Man and Cybernetics, Yasmine Hammamet, Tunisia; Tunisia; 2002

[11] Arslan A, Kaya M. Determination of fuzzy logic membership functions using genetic algorithms. Fuzzy Sets and Systems. 2001;**118**(2):297-306

[12] Zhang W, Liu Y. Fuzzy logic controlled particle swarm for reactive power optimization considering voltage stability. In: The 7th International Conference on Power Engineering; Singapore; January 2005. DOI: 10.1109/IPEC.2005.206969

Chapter 2

Fuzzy Information Measures with Multiple Parameters

Anjali Munde

Additional information is available at the end of the chapter

http://dx.doi.org/10.5772/intechopen.78803

Abstract

Information theory deals with the study of problems concerning any system. This includes information processing, information storage, information retrieval and decision making. Information theory studies all theoretical problems connected with the transmission of information over communication channels. This includes the study of uncertainty (information) measures and various practical and economical methods of coding information for transmission. In this chapter, the introduction of a new generalised measure of fuzzy information involving two real parameters is given. The proposed measure satisfies all the necessary properties of being a measure. Some additional properties of the proposed measure have also been studied. Further, the monotonic nature of generalised fuzzy information measure with respect to the parameters is studied and validity of the same is checked by constructing the computed tables and plots on taking different fuzzy sets and different values of the parameters. Also, a new generalised fuzzy information measure involving three parameters has been introduced.

Keywords: fuzzy set theory, entropy, fuzzy information measures, monotonicity, symmetry

1. Background

Shannon [1] introduced the concept of entropy in communication theory and founded the subject of information theory. The stochastic system has an important property known as entropy which is widely used in various fields.

Further, the second law of thermodynamics that explains that there cannot be spontaneous decrease in the entropy of system described that over time the systems tend to be more disordered. Thus, information theory has found wide applications in statistics, information processing and computing instead of concerned with communication systems only.

If we consider entropy equivalent to uncertainty then an enormous deal of insight can be obtained. Zadeh [2] introduced and enlightened about a generalised theory of vagueness or ambiguity. In order to observe about the external world, uncertainty plays a very important role. For understanding composite phenomena, any discipline that contributes in order to understand measure, regulate, maximise or minimise and control is considered as a significant input.

Uncertainty plays a significant role in our perceptions about the external world. Any discipline that can assist us in understanding it, measuring it, regulating it, maximizing or minimizing it and ultimately controlling it to the extent possible, should certainly be considered an important contribution to our scientific understanding of complex phenomena.

Uncertainty is not a single monolithic concept. It can appear in several guises. It can arise in what we normally consider a probabilistic phenomenon. On the other hand, it can also appear in a deterministic phenomenon where we know that the outcome is not a chance event, but we are fuzzy about the possibility of the specific outcome. This type of uncertainty arising out of fuzziness is the subject of investigation of the relatively new discipline of fuzzy set theory.

We shall first take up the case of probabilistic uncertainty. Probabilistic uncertainty is related to the uncertainty connected with the probability of outcomes.

Consider a set of events $E = (E_1, E_2,..., En)$ with a set of probability distribution $P = (p_1, p_2, ..., p_n)$, $p_i \geq 0$, $\sum_{i=1}^{n} p_i = 1$.

Then the Shannon [1] entropy associated with P is given by,

$$H(P) = -\sum_{i=1}^{n} p_i \log p_i \tag{1}$$

The base of logarithm is taken as 2. Also it is assumed that

$$0 \log 0 = 0.$$

Shannon [1] obtained (Eq. (1)) on the basis of following postulates:

1. H(P) should be a continuous permutationally symmetric function of $p_1, p_2,..., p_n$, that is, ambiguity changes by slight quantity if there is slight quantity changes in p_i's and ambiguity remain unchanged if p_i's exchange among themselves.

2. $H(p_1, p_2,..., p_n, 0) = H(p_1, p_2,..., p_n)$, that is, uncertainty should not change when an impossible outcome is added to the scheme.

3. H(P) should be minimum when P is any one of the n degenerate distribution $\Delta_1 = (1, 0, ..., 0)$, $\Delta_2 = (0, 1, ..., 0), ..., \Delta_n = (0, 0, ..., 1)$ and the minimum value should be zero because in all these cases, there is no uncertainty about the outcome.

4. H(P) should be maximum when $p_1 = p_2 = ... = p_n = 1/n$ because in this case the uncertainty is maximum.

5. $H(P*Q) = H(P) + H(Q)$, that is, the uncertainty of two independent probability distributions is the sum of the uncertainties of the two probability distributions.

6. $H(p_1, p_2,..., p_n) = H(p_1 + p_2, p_3,..., p_n) + (p_1 + p_2)H(p_1/p_1 + p_2, p_2/p_1 + p_2)$

The measures in (Eq. (1)) not only measures uncertainty, but it also measures equality of p_1, p_2, ..., p_n, since it has the maximum value when p_1, p_2,...,p_n, are all equal and has the minimum value when p_i's are most unequal. In fact p_i's can be regarded as proportions rather than probabilities.

After Shannon's [1] entropy, various other measures of entropy have been proposed.

Entropy of order α was described by Renyi [3] in the way as:

$$H_\alpha(P) = \frac{1}{1-\alpha} \left(\log \left(\sum_{i=1}^n p_i^\alpha \Big/ \sum_{i=1}^n p_i \right) \right), \alpha \neq 1, \alpha > 0 \tag{2}$$

Entropy of order α and type β was described by Kapur in the way as:

$$H_{\alpha,\beta}(P) = \frac{1}{1-\alpha} \log \left(\sum_{i=1}^n p_i^{\alpha+\beta-1} \Big/ \sum_{i=1}^n p_i^\beta \right), \alpha \neq 1, \alpha > 0, \beta > 0, \alpha + \beta - 1 > 0 \tag{3}$$

Havrada and Charvat [4] gave the first nonadditive measure of entropy and it is used in the modified form as

$$H^\alpha(P) = \frac{1}{1-\alpha} \left(\sum_{i=1}^n p_i^\alpha - 1 \right), \alpha \neq 1, \alpha > 0. \tag{4}$$

Behara and Chawla [5] defined the nonadditive τ entropy as

$$H_\tau(P) = \frac{1 - \left(\sum_{i=1}^n p_i^{\frac{1}{\tau}} \right)^\tau}{1 - 2^{\tau-1}}, \tau \neq 1, \tau > 0. \tag{5}$$

Kapur [6] gave the following nonadditive measures of entropy:

$$H_a(P) = -\sum_{i=1}^n p_i \log p_i + \frac{1}{a} \sum_{i=1}^n [(1 + ap_i) \log (1 + ap_i) - ap_i], a > 0 \tag{6}$$

$$H_b(P) = -\sum_{i=1}^n p_i \log p_i + \frac{1}{b} \sum_{i=1}^n [(1 + bp_i) \log (1 + bp_i) - (1 + b) \log (1 + b)p_i], b > 0 \tag{7}$$

$$H_c(P) = -\sum_{i=1}^n p_i \log p_i + \frac{1}{c^2} \sum_{i=1}^n [(1 + cp_i) \log (1 + cp_i) - cp_i], c > 0 \tag{8}$$

$$H_k(P) = -\sum_{i=1}^n p_i \log p_i + \frac{1}{k^2} \sum_{i=1}^n [(1 + kp_i) \log (1 + kp_i) - (1 + k) \log (1 + k)p_i], k > 0 \tag{9}$$

2. Technical aspects of fuzzy measures

Zadeh [2] introduced fuzzy set theory which is associated with vagueness arising in human cognitive methods. The alteration for an element connecting membership and nonmembership in the universe of classical sets is abrupt whereas in the universe of fuzzy sets the transition is gradual. Thus, the membership function describes the vagueness and ambiguity of an element and takes values in the interval [0, 1].

Kapur [7] explained the concept of fuzzy entropy by considering the following vector $\{\mu_A(x_1), \mu_A(x_2), ..., \mu_A(x_n)\}$.

If $\mu_A(x_i) = 0$ then the ith element does not belong to set A and if $\mu_A(x_i) = 1$, then the ith element belongs to set A. If $\mu_A(x_i) = 0.5$ then highest ambiguity arises as to i^{th} element belongs to set A or not. Thus, $\{\mu_A(x_1), \mu_A(x_2), ..., \mu_A(x_n)\}$ is termed as fuzzy vector and the set A is identified as the fuzzy set. Thus crisp set are those sets in which each element is 0 or 1 and hence uncertainty does not arise in these sets whereas those sets in which elements are 0 or 1 and others lie among 0 and 1 are entitled as fuzzy sets. A fuzzy set A is represented as A = $\left\{ x_i/\mu_A(x_i); i = 1, 2, ..., n \right\}$ where $\mu_A(x_i)$ gives the degree of belongingness of the element (x_i) to A. We explain the concept of membership function $\mu_A: X \rightarrow [0, 1]$ as follows:

$$\mu_A(x_i) = \left\{ \begin{array}{l} 0, \ if \ x \notin A \ and \ there \ is \ no \ ambiguity \\ 1, \ if \ x \in A \ and \ there \ is \ no \ ambiguity \\ 0.5, \ if \ there \ is \ maximum \ ambiguity \ whether \ x \notin A \ x \in A \end{array} \right\} \quad (10)$$

Further if $\mu_B(x_i) = \mu_A(x_i)$ either $1 - \mu_A(x_i)$ or then fuzzy sets A and B are characterised as fuzzy equivalent sets. Also, without being fuzzy equivalent, two sets can have same entropy but it is obvious to have identical entropy for fuzzy equivalent sets. Now if all the membership values of class of fuzzy equivalent sets are less than or equal to 0.5 then that set is defined as standard fuzzy set.

For any fuzzy set A* to be a sharpened version of set A the subsequent requirements has to be fulfilled:

$$\mu_{A^*}(x_i) \leq \mu_A(x_i), if \ \mu_A(x_i) \leq 0.5; \forall i \quad (11)$$

and

$$\mu_{A^*}(x_i) \geq \mu_A(x_i), if \mu_A(x_i) \geq 0.5; \forall i \quad (12)$$

Thus, when $x_1, x_2, ..., x_n$ are components of universe of discourse then, $\{\mu_A(x_1), \mu_A(x_2), ..., \mu_A(x_n)\}$ are positioned among 0 and 1 but since their sum is not unity therefore they are not considered as probabilities. However,

$$\phi_A(x_i) = \frac{\mu_A(x_i)}{\sum_{i=1}^{n} \mu_A(x_i)}, \quad i = 1, 2, ..., n \quad (13)$$

gives a probability distribution.

With the ith element, fuzzy uncertainty is defined as $f(\mu_A(x_i))$ with the following properties:

1. $f(x) = 0$ when $x = 0$ or 1.

2. $f(x)$ increases as x goes from 0 to 0.5.

3. $f(x)$ decreases as x goes from 0.5 to 1.

4. $f(x) = f(1 - x)$.

The total fuzzy uncertainty defined as fuzzy entropy for n independent elements is given by,

$$H(A) = \sum_{i=1}^{n} f(\mu_A(x_i)) \tag{14}$$

This is called fuzzy entropy.

When there is uncertainty due to fuzziness of information it is known as fuzzy entropy measures whereas when the uncertainty is due to information available in terms of probability distribution it is known as probabilistic entropy. Following similarities and dissimilarities are there between fuzzy entropy measures and probabilistic entropy measures:

1. $0 \le p_i \le 1$ for each i. Also $0 \le (\mu_A(x_i)) \le 1$ for each i.

2. $\sum_{i=1}^{n} p_i = 1$ for all probability distributions, but $\sum_{i=1}^{n} (\mu_A(x_i))$ need not be equal to unity and it need not even be the same for all fuzzy sets.

3. The probabilistic uncertainty measure measures how close the probability distribution (p_1, p_2, ..., p_n) is to the uniform distribution (1/n, 1/n, ..., 1/n) and how far away it is from degenerate distributions. Fuzzy uncertainty measures how close the fuzzy distribution is from the most fuzzy vector distribution (1/2, 1/2, ..., 1/2) and how far it is from the distribution of crisp sets.

4. $(\mu_A(x_i))$ gives the same degree of fuzziness as $1 - (\mu_A(x_i))$ because both are equidistant from 1/2 and the crisp set values 0 and 1. However probabilities p and $1 - p$ make different contributions to probabilistic uncertainty. As such while most measures of fuzzy entropy are of the form $\sum_{i=1}^{n} f(\mu_A(x_i) + \sum_{i=1}^{n} f(1 - \mu_A(x_i))$, most measures of probabilities entropy are of the form $\sum_{i=1}^{n} f(p_i)$. However some measures of probabilistic entropy can also be of the form $\sum_{i=1}^{n} f(p_i) + \sum_{i=1}^{n} f(p_i)$.

5. Similarly while many measures for fuzzy directed divergence are all of the form $\sum_{i=1}^{n} f(\mu_A(x_i), \mu_B(x_i) + \sum_{i=1}^{n} f(1 - \mu_A(x_i)), (1 - \mu_B(x_i)))$, most of the probabilistic measures are of the form $\sum_{i=1}^{n} f(p_i, q_i)$. For each measure of probabilistic entropy or directed divergence, we have a corresponding measure of fuzzy entropy and fuzzy directed divergence and vice-versa.

6. The common properties arise from the consideration that both types of measures are based on measures of distance from (1/n, 1/n, ..., 1/n) in one case and from (1/2, 1/2, ..., 1/2) in the other.

7. The dissimilarity arises because while $\sum_{i=1}^{n} p_i = 1$, $\sum_{i=1}^{n} \left(\mu_A(x_i) \right.$ is not 1. The probabilities of n − 1 outcomes will determine the probability of the nth outcome. However fuzziness of n elements of the fuzzy set are quite independent and our knowledge of fuzziness of n − 1 elements gives us no information about the fuzziness of the nth element.

8. Conceptually the two types of uncertainty are poles apart. One deals with probabilities or relative frequencies and repeated experiments, while the other deals with estimation of fuzzy values. The probabilities can be determined objectively and experimentally and should naturally be the same for everyone. Fuzziness is one's perception of membership of an element of a set and can be subjective. However, after finding fuzzy value for every member of the set, everything else is objective. In probability theory also after assigning probabilities, everything is also objective.

9. Fuzzy and probabilistic entropies are concave functions of $\{\mu_A(x_1), \mu_A(x_2), ..., \mu_A(x_n)\}$ and $p_1, p_2, ..., p_n$ respectively. If we start with any value of $\{\mu_A(x_1), \mu_A(x_2), ..., \mu_A(x_n)\}$ and approach the vector 1/2, 1/2, ..., 1/2, the fuzzy entropy will increase. Similarly, if we start with any probability vector $p_1, p_2, ..., p_n$ and approach the vector 1/n, 1/n, ..., 1/n, the probabilistic entropy will increase. Thus, $Z = F\{\mu_A(x_1), \mu_A(x_2), ..., \mu_A(x_n)\}$, where F is a fuzzy entropy is a concave surface with maximum value at 1/2, 1/2, ..., 1/2. Similarly Z = G($p_1, p_2, ..., p_n$) where G is probabilistic entropy is a concave surface with maximum value at 1/n, 1/n, ..., 1/n.

While processing information, making decision and in our language we can find fuzziness. Many authentic world objectives and human thinking consider uncertainty and fuzziness as their fundamental nature. Uncertainty and fuzziness are removed by the utilization of information. The degree of information is the quantity of uncertainty eliminated whereas the degree of vagueness and ambiguity of uncertainties is the quantity of fuzziness.

The theory of fuzziness is related to various areas of research such as Statistics, Information theory, Clustering and Decision analysis, Medical and Socio-economic prediction, Image processing, etc. The preparation and analysis of information development method are the applications of the mathematical designs related to system research.

In order to deal with fuzziness there is a small area from the extremely large fields of theories and applications which have been developed from the concept of fuzziness.

We define problems in the form of decision, management and prediction and by analysis, understanding and utilization of information, we can find their solutions. Thus, a significant quantity of information together with significant quantity of uncertainty is considered as the ground of many problems.

As we become aware of how much we know and how much we do not know, as information and uncertainty themselves become the focus of our concern, we begin to see our problems as centring on the issue of complexity.

Thus, ambiguity due to fuzziness of information is calculated by fuzzy entropy whereas vagueness due to information which is accessible in context of probability distribution is computed by probabilistic entropy.

Entropy theory was developed to measure uncertainty of a probability distribution and therefore it was natural for researchers in fuzzy set theory to make use of entropy concepts in measuring fuzziness.

Entropy of a fuzzy set A having n support points was characterised by Kauffman [8] in the way as

$$H_k(A) = -\frac{1}{\log n} \sum_{i=1}^{n} \phi_A(x_i) \log \phi_A(x_i) \tag{15}$$

Deluca and Termini [9] suggested the measure

$$H_D(A) = -\frac{1}{n \log 2} \sum_{i=1}^{n} [\mu_A(x_i) \log \mu_A(x_i) + (1 - \mu_A(x_i)) \log (1 - \mu_A(x_i))] \tag{16}$$

Bhandari and Pal [10] suggested the following measure:

$$H_e(A) = \frac{1}{n\sqrt{e}-1} \sum \log \left[\mu_A(x_i) e^{1-\mu_A(x_i)} + (1 - \mu_A(x_i)) e^{\mu_A(x_i)} - 1 \right] \tag{17}$$

Some other measures of fuzzy entropy are:

1. Corresponding to Sharma and Taneja's [11] measure of entropy of degree α, β

$$H_\alpha^\beta(P) = \frac{1}{\beta - \alpha} \left[\sum_{i=1}^{n} p_i^\alpha - \sum_{i=1}^{n} p_i^\beta \right], \quad \alpha \neq \beta \tag{18}$$

we get the measure

$$H_\alpha^\beta(A) = \frac{1}{\beta - \alpha} \sum_{i=1}^{n} \left[\mu_A^\alpha(x_i) + (1 - \mu_A(x_i))^\alpha - \mu_A^\beta(x_i) + (1 - \mu_A(x_i))^\beta \right] \tag{19}$$

where either $\alpha \geq 1$, $\beta \leq 1$ or $\alpha \leq 1$, $\beta \geq 1$ and $\alpha = \beta$ only if both are unity.

2. Corresponding to Kapur's measure of entropy of degree α, β

$$H_\alpha^\beta(P) = \frac{1}{\alpha + \beta - 2} \left[\sum_{i=1}^{n} p_i^\alpha + \sum_{i=1}^{n} p_i^\beta - 2 \right] \tag{20}$$

we get the measure

$$H_\alpha^\beta(A) = \frac{1}{\alpha + \beta - 2} \sum_{i=1}^n \left[\mu_A^\alpha(x_i) + \left(1 - \mu_A(x_i)\right)^\alpha - \mu_A^\beta(x_i) + \left(1 - \mu_A(x_i)\right)^\beta - 2 \right] \qquad (21)$$

3. Corresponding to Kapur's [12] measure of entropy

$$H_a(P) = - \sum_{i=1}^n p_i \ \log p_i + \frac{1}{a} \sum_{i=1}^n \left[(1 + a p_i) \log (1 + a p_i) - \frac{1}{a}(1 + a) \log (1 + a) \right], a \geq 0 \qquad (22)$$

we get the measure

$$H_a(A) = - \sum_{i=1}^n \left[\mu_A(x_i) \log \mu_A(x_i) + \left(1 - \mu_A(x_i)\right) \log \left(1 - \mu_A(x_i)\right) \right]$$

$$+ \frac{1}{a} \sum_{i=1}^n \left[\left(1 + a \mu_A(x_i)\right) \log \left(1 + a \mu_A(x_i)\right) \right] + \frac{1}{a} \sum_{i=1}^n \left[(1 + a - a \mu_A(x_i)) \log \left(1 + a - a \mu_A(x_i)\right) \right]$$

$$- \frac{1}{a}(1 - a) \log (1 - a)$$

$$(23)$$

4. Corresponding to Kapur's [4] measure of entropy of degree α and type β

$$H^{\alpha, \beta}(P) = \frac{1}{\beta - \alpha} \log \frac{\sum_{i=1}^n p_i^\alpha}{\sum_{i=1}^n p_i^\beta}, \alpha \neq \beta \qquad (24)$$

we get the measure

$$H^{\alpha, \beta}(P) = \frac{1}{\beta - \alpha} \log \frac{\sum_{i=1}^n \mu_A^\alpha(x_i) + \left(1 - \mu_A^\alpha(x_i)\right)^\alpha}{\sum_{i=1}^n \mu_A^\beta(x_i) + \left(1 - \mu_A(x_i)\right)^\beta}, \alpha \geq 1, \beta \leq 1 \quad or \ \alpha \leq 1, \beta \geq 1. \qquad (25)$$

Kosko [13] introduced fuzzy entropy and conditioning. Pal and Pal [14] gave object background segmentation using new definition of entropy. Parkash [15] proposed new measures of weighted fuzzy entropy and their applications for the study of maximum weighted fuzzy entropy principle. Parkash and Gandhi [16] suggested new generalised measures of fuzzy entropy and properties. Parkash and Singh [17] gave characterization of useful information theoretic measures. Taneja [18] introduced generalised information measures and their applications. Taneja and Tuteja [19] gave characterization of quantitative-qualitative measure of relative information. Tuteja [20] introduced characterization of nonadditive measures of relative information and accuracy. Tuteja and Hooda [21] proposed generalised useful information measure of type α and degree β. Tuteja and Jain [22, 23] gave characterization of relative useful information having utilities as monotone functions and an axiomatic characterization of relative useful information. Tahayori [24] presented a universal methodology for generating an interval type 2 fuzzy set membership function from a collection of type 1 fuzzy sets. Kumar and Bajaj [25] introduced NTV metric based entropies of interval-valued intuitionistic fuzzy sets and their applications in decision making.

Mishra [26] introduced two exponential fuzzy information measures and characterised axiomatically. To show the effectiveness of the proposed measure, it is compared with the existing measures. Further, two fuzzy discrimination and symmetric discrimination measures are defined and their validity are checked. Important properties of new measures are studied and their applications in pattern recognition and diagnosis problem of crop disease are discussed. Hooda and Mishra [27] gave two sine and cosine trigonometric measures of fuzzy information and obtained new measures of trigonometric fuzzy information.

3. A new parametric measure of fuzzy information measure involving two parameters α and β

A new generalised fuzzy information measure of order α and type β has been suggested and their necessary and required properties are examined. Thereafter, its validity is also verified. Also, the monotonic behaviour of fuzzy information measure of order α and type β has been conferred.

The generalised measure of fuzzy information of order α and type β is given by,

$$H_\alpha^\beta(A) = \frac{1}{(1-\alpha)\beta} \sum_{i=1}^{n} \left[\left(\mu_A^{\alpha\mu_A(x_i)} + (1 - \mu_A(x_i))^{\alpha(1-\mu_A(x_i))} \right)^\beta - 2^\beta \right],$$

$$\alpha > 0, \alpha \neq 1, \beta \neq 0.$$

(26)

3.1. Properties of $H_\alpha^\beta(A)$

We have supposed that, $0^{0.\alpha} = 1$, we study the following properties:

Property 1: $H_\alpha^\beta(A) \geq 0$ i.e. $H_\alpha^\beta(A)$ is nonnegative.

Property 2: $H_\alpha^\beta(A)$ is minimum if A is a non-fuzzy set.

For $\mu_A(x_i) = 0$, it implies $H_\alpha^\beta(A) = 0$ and $\mu_A(x_i) = 0$ we have $H_\alpha^\beta(A) = 0$.

Property 3: $H_\alpha^\beta(A)$ is maximum if A is most fuzzy set.

We have, $\frac{\partial H_\alpha^\beta(A)}{\partial \mu_A(x_i)} = \frac{\alpha}{1-\alpha} \left[\{\mu_A(x_i)\}^{\alpha\mu_A(x_i)} + \{1 - \mu_A(x_i)\}^{\alpha(1-\mu_A(x_i))} \right]^{\beta-1} \left[\{\mu_A(x_i)\}^{\alpha\mu_A(x_i)} (1 + \log \mu_A(x_i)) - \{1 - \mu_A(x_i)\}^{\alpha(1-\mu_A(x_i))} (1 + \log (1 - \mu_A(x_i))) \right]$.

Taking, $\frac{\partial H_\alpha^\beta(A)}{\partial \mu_A(x_i)} = 0$ which is possible $\mu_A(x_i) = 1 - \mu_A(x_i)$ that is if $\mu_A(x_i) = \frac{1}{2}$.

Now, we have, $\frac{\partial^2 H_\alpha^\beta(A)}{\partial^2 \mu_A(x_i)}$, Thus, at $\mu_A(x_i) = \frac{1}{2}$.

$$\frac{\partial^2 H_\alpha^\beta(A)}{\partial^2 \mu_A(x_i)} = \frac{-1}{1-\frac{1}{\alpha}}(2^{1-\frac{\alpha}{2}})^{\beta-1}\left[2^{2-\frac{\alpha}{2}} + \alpha.2^{1-\frac{\alpha}{2}}(1 - \log 2)^2 < 0\right]$$

Hence, the maximum value exists at $\mu_A(x_i) = \frac{1}{2}$.

Property 4: $H_\alpha^\beta(A^*) \leq H_\alpha^\beta(A)$, where A^* be sharpened version of A.

When $\mu_A(x_i) = \frac{1}{2}$,

$$H_\alpha^\beta(A) = \frac{n.2^\beta}{(1-\alpha)\beta}\left(\frac{1 - 2^{\frac{\alpha\beta}{2}}}{2^{\frac{\alpha\beta}{2}}}\right)$$

When $\mu_A(x_i)$ lies between 0 and 1/2 then $H_\alpha^\beta(A)$ is an increasing function whereas when $\mu_A(x_i)$ lies between 1/2 and 1 then $H_\alpha^\beta(A)$ is a decreasing function of $\mu_A(x_i)$

Let A^* be sharpened version of A which means that

i.   If $\mu_A(x_i) < 0.5$ then $\mu_{A^*}(x_i) \leq \mu_A(x_i)$ for all i = 1, 2, ..., n

ii.   If $\mu_A(x_i) > 0.5$ then $\mu_{A^*}(x_i) \geq \mu_A(x_i)$ for all i = 1, 2, ..., n

Since $H_\alpha^\beta(A)$ is an increasing function of $\mu_A(x_i)$ for $0 \leq \mu_A(x_i) \leq \frac{1}{2}$ and decreasing function of $\mu_A(x_i)$ for $\frac{1}{2} \leq \mu_A(x_i) \leq 1$, therefore

i. $\mu_{A^*}(x_i) \leq \mu_A(x_i)$ this implies $H_\alpha^\beta(A^*) \leq H_\alpha^\beta(A)$ in [0, 0.5]

ii. $\mu_{A^*}(x_i) \leq \mu_A(x_i)$ this implies $H_\alpha^\beta(A^*) \leq H_\alpha^\beta(A)$ in [0.5, 1]

Hence, $H_\alpha^\beta(A^*) \leq H_\alpha^\beta(A)$.

Property 5: $H_\alpha^\beta(A) = H_\alpha^\beta(\overline{A})$, where $\overline{A}$ is the compliment of A i.e. $\mu_A(x_i) = 1 - \mu_A(x_i)$.

Thus when $\mu_A(x_i)$ is varied to $(1 - \mu_A(x_i))$ then $H_\alpha^\beta(A)$ does not change.

Under the above conditions, the generalised measure proposed in (26) is a valid measure of fuzzy information measure.

3.2. Monotonic behaviour of fuzzy information measure

In this section we study the monotonic behaviour of the fuzzy information measure. For this, diverse values of $H_\alpha^\beta(A)$ by assigning various values to α and β has been calculated and further the generalised measure has been presented graphically.

Case I: For $\alpha > 1$, $\beta = 1$, we have compiled the values of $H_\alpha^\beta(A)$ in **Table 1**, (a) and presented the fuzzy entropy in **Figure 1(a)** which unambiguously illustrates that the fuzzy information measure is a concave function.

For $\alpha = 2$, $\beta = 1$, values of $H_\alpha^\beta(A)$ have been represented with the help of graph for $\alpha = 2$ and $\beta = 1$ which implies that the proposed measure is a concave function. Similarly, for other values of α and β, we get different concave curves.

$\mu_A(x_i)$	$H_\alpha^\beta(A)$	$\mu_A(x_i)$	$H_\alpha^\beta(A)$	$\mu_A(x_i)$	$H_\alpha^\beta(A)$
0.0	0.0	0.0	0.0	0.0	0.0
0.1	0.5419	0.1	0.5074	0.1	2.0337
0.2	0.7749	0.2	0.7763	0.2	2.7289
0.3	0.9075	0.3	0.9534	0.3	3.0732
0.4	0.9778	0.4	1.0517	0.4	3.2411
0.5	1.0	0.5	1.0844	0.5	3.2916
0.6	0.9778	0.6	1.0517	0.6	3.2411
0.7	0.9075	0.7	0.9534	0.7	3.0732
0.8	0.7749	0.8	0.7763	0.8	2.7289
0.9	0.5419	0.9	0.5074	0.9	2.0337
1.0	0.0	1.0	0.0	1.0	0.0
(a)		(b)		(c)	

Table 1. The values of fuzzy information measure for $\alpha = 2$ and $\beta = 1$; $\alpha = 1.5$ and $\beta = 0.1$; and $\alpha = 1.5$ and $\beta = 2.5$.

Case II: For $\alpha > 1$, $0 < \beta < 1$ we have compiled the values of $H_\alpha^\beta(A)$ in **Table 1,** (b) and presented the fuzzy entropy in the **Figure 1(b)** which unambiguously illustrates that the fuzzy entropy is a concave function.

For $\alpha = 1.5$ and $\beta = 0.1$, values of $H_\alpha^\beta(A)$ have been represented with the help of graph for $\alpha = 1.5$ and $\beta = 0.1$ which implies that the proposed measure is a concave function. Similarly, for other values of α and β, we get different concave curves.

Case III: For $\alpha > 1$, $\beta > 1$ we have compiled the values of $H_\alpha^\beta(A)$ in **Table 1,** (c) and presented the fuzzy entropy in **Figure 1(c)** which unambiguously illustrates that the fuzzy entropy is a concave function.

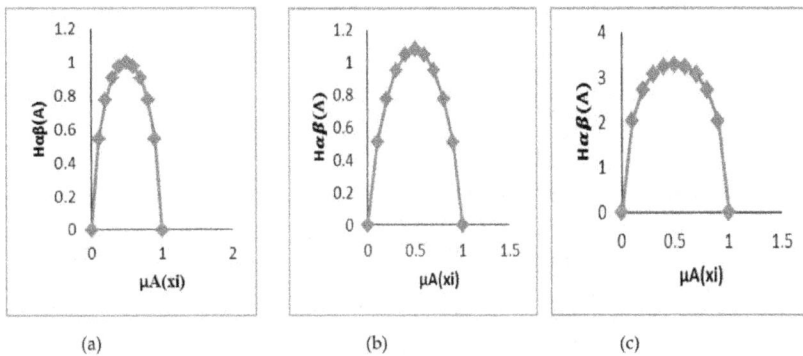

Figure 1. Representation of the monotonic behaviour of fuzzy information measure for (a) For, $\alpha = 2$ and $\beta = 1$; (b) For, $\alpha = 1.5$ and $\beta = 0.1$; and (C) For, $\alpha = 1.5$ and $\beta = 2.5$.

For $\alpha = 1.5$ and $\beta = 2.5$, values of $H_\alpha^\beta(A)$ have been represented with the help of graph for $\alpha = 1.5$ and $\beta = 2.5$ which implies that the proposed measure is a concave function. Similarly, for other values of α and β, we get different concave curves.

4. A new parametric measure of fuzzy information measure involving three parameters α, β and γ

Further, a new generalised fuzzy information measure involving three parameters α, β and γ has been suggested and their necessary and required properties are examined. Thereafter, its validity is also verified. Also, the monotonic behaviour of fuzzy information measure of order α, β and γ has been introduced.

The generalised measure of fuzzy information involving three parameters α, β and γ is given by,

$$H_{\alpha,\beta,\gamma}(A) = \frac{1}{1-\alpha} \sum_{i=1}^{n} \left[\left(\mu_A^{(\alpha+\beta)\mu_A(x_i)} + \left(1 - \mu_A(x_i)\right)^{(\alpha+\beta)(1-\mu_A(x_i))} \right)^\gamma - 2^\gamma \right],$$

(27)

$$\alpha > 0, \alpha \neq 1, \beta \neq 0, \gamma \neq 0$$

4.1. Properties of $H_{\alpha,\beta,\gamma}(A)$

We have supposed that, $0^{0.\alpha} = 1$, we study the following properties:

Property 1: $H_{\alpha,\beta,\gamma}(A) \geq 0$ i.e. $H_{\alpha,\beta,\gamma}(A)$ is nonnegative.

Property 2: $H_{\alpha,\beta,\gamma}(A)$ is minimum if A is a non-fuzzy set.

for $\mu_A(x_i) = 0$, it implies $H_{\alpha,\beta,\gamma}(A) = 0$ and $\mu_A(x_i) = 1$ we have $H_{\alpha,\beta,\gamma}(A) = 0$.

Property 3: $H_{\alpha,\beta,\gamma}(A^*) \leq H_{\alpha,\beta,\gamma}(A)$, where A^* be sharpened version of A.

When $\mu_A(x_i)$ lies between 0 and 1/2 then $H_{\alpha,\beta,\gamma}(A)$ is an increasing function whereas when $\mu_A(x_i)$ lies between 1/2 and 1 then $H_{\alpha,\beta,\gamma}(A)$ is a decreasing function of $\mu_A(x_i)$

Let A^* be sharpened version of A which means that

i.   If $\mu_A(x_i) < 0.5$ then $\mu_{A^*}(x_i) \leq \mu_A(x_i)$ for all i = 1, 2, ..., n

ii.   If $\mu_A(x_i) > 0.5$ then $\mu_{A^*}(x_i) \geq \mu_A(x_i)$ for all i = 1, 2, ..., n

Since $H_{\alpha,\beta,\gamma}(A)$ is an increasing function of $\mu_A(x_i)$ for $0 \leq \mu_A(x_i) \leq \frac{1}{2}$ and decreasing function of $\mu_A(x_i)$ for $\frac{1}{2} \leq \mu_A(x_i) \leq 1$, therefore

i. $\mu_{A^*}(x_i) \leq \mu_A(x_i)$ this implies $H_{\alpha,\beta,\gamma}(A^*) \leq H_{\alpha,\beta,\gamma}(A)$ in [0, 0.5]

ii. $\mu_{A^*}(x_i) \leq \mu_A(x_i)$ this implies $H_{\alpha,\beta,\gamma}(A^*) \leq H_{\alpha,\beta,\gamma}(A)$ in [0.5, 1]

Hence, $H_{\alpha,\beta,\gamma}(A^*) \leq H_{\alpha,\beta,\gamma}(A)$

Property 4: $H_{\alpha,\beta,\gamma}(A) = H_{\alpha,\beta,\gamma}(\overline{A})$, where $(\overline{A})$ is the compliment of A i.e. $\mu_A(x_i) = 1 - \mu_A(x_i)$

Thus, when $\mu_A(x_i)$ is varied to $1 - \mu_A(x_i)$ then $H_{\alpha,\beta,\gamma}(A)$ does not change.

Under the above conditions, the generalised measure proposed in (27) is a valid measure of fuzzy information measure.

4.2. Monotonic behaviour of fuzzy information measure

In this section we study the monotonic behaviour of the fuzzy information measure. For this, diverse values of $H_{\alpha,\beta,\gamma}(A)$ by assigning various values to α, β and γ have been calculated and further the generalised measure has been presented graphically.

Case I: For $\alpha > 1$, $\beta = 2$, $\gamma = 3$, we have compiled the values of $H_{\alpha,\beta,\gamma}(A)$ in **Table 2**, (a)–(e) and presented the fuzzy entropy in **Figure 2(a)–(e)** which unambiguously illustrates that the fuzzy information measure is a concave function. For $\alpha = 1.5$, $\beta = 2$, $\gamma = 3$, values of $H_{\alpha,\beta,\gamma}(A)$ have been represented with the help of graph $\gamma = 3$ which implies that the proposed measure is a concave function. Similarly, for other values of α, β and γ we get different concave curves. Further it has been shown that $H_{\alpha,\beta,\gamma}(A)$ is a concave function obtaining its maximum value at $\mu_A(x_i) = \frac{1}{2}$. Hence $H_{\alpha,\beta,\gamma}(A)$ is increasing function of $\mu_A(x_i)$ in interval [0, 0.5) and decreasing function of $\mu_A(x_i)$ in interval (0.5, 1]. Similarly, for $\alpha = 2$, $\beta = 2$ and $\gamma = 3$, $\alpha = 2.5$, $\beta = 2$ and $\gamma = 3$, $\alpha = 3$, $\beta = 2$ and $\gamma = 3$, $\alpha = 3.5$, $\beta = 2$ and $\gamma = 3$, $\gamma = 3$ values of $H_{\alpha,\beta,\gamma}(A)$ have been represented with the help of graph which implies that the proposed measure is a concave function.

$\mu_A(x_i)$	$H_{\alpha,\beta,\gamma}(A)$	$\mu_A(x_i)$	$H_{\alpha,\beta,\gamma}(A)$	$\mu_A(x_i)$	$H_{\alpha,\beta,\gamma}(A)$	$\mu_A(x_i)$	$H_{\alpha,\beta,\gamma}(A)$	$\mu_A(x_i)$	$H_{\alpha,\beta,\gamma}(A)$
0.0	0.0	0.0	0.0	0.0	0.0	0.0	0.0	0.0	0.0
0.1	12.8444	0.1	6.7318	0.1	4.6517	0.1	3.5865	0.1	2.9316
0.2	14.7302	0.2	7.5514	0.2	5.1212	0.2	3.8867	0.2	3.1353
0.3	15.3147	0.3	7.7794	0.3	5.2385	0.3	3.9540	0.3	3.1762
0.4	15.5250	0.4	7.8559	0.4	5.2750	0.4	3.9734	0.4	3.1870
0.5	15.5795	0.5	7.875	0.5	5.2837	0.5	3.9779	0.5	3.1894
0.6	15.5250	0.6	7.8559	0.6	5.2750	0.6	3.9734	0.6	3.1870
0.7	15.3147	0.7	7.7794	0.7	5.2385	0.7	3.9540	0.7	3.1762
0.8	14.7302	0.8	7.5514	0.8	5.1212	0.8	3.8867	0.8	3.1353
0.9	12.8444	0.9	6.7318	0.9	4.6517	0.9	3.5865	0.9	2.9316
1.0	0.0	1.0	0.0	1.0	0.0	1.0	0.0	1.0	0.0
(a)		(b)		(c)		(d)		(e)	

Table 2. The values of fuzzy information measure for $\alpha = 1.5$, $\beta = 2$ and $\gamma = 3$; $\alpha = 2$, $\beta = 2$ and $\gamma = 3$; $\alpha = 2.5$, $\beta = 2$ and $\gamma = 3$; $\alpha = 3$, $\beta = 2$ and $\gamma = 3$; and $\alpha = 3.5$, $\beta = 2$ and $\gamma = 3$.

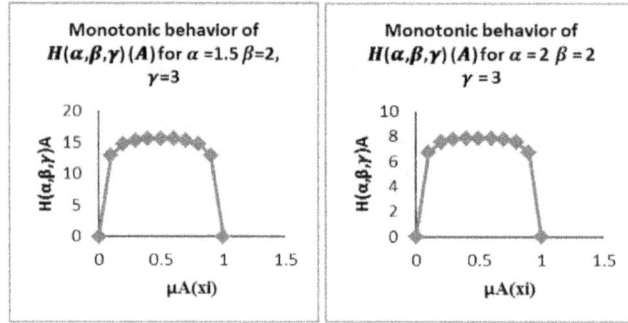

(a)   (b)

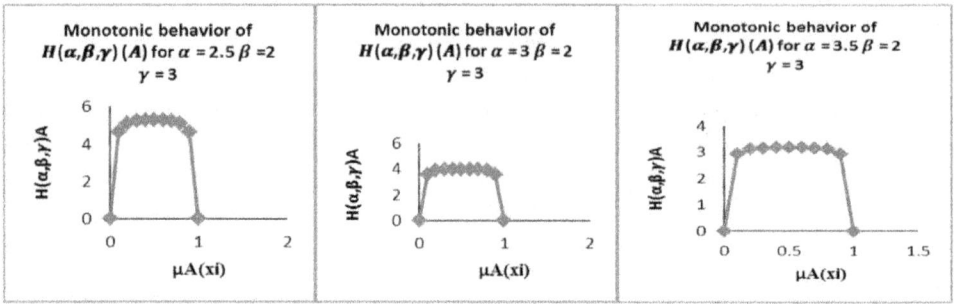

(c)   (d)   (e)

Figure 2. Representation of the monotonic behaviour of fuzzy information measure for (a) For, $\alpha = 1.5$, $\beta = 2$ and $\gamma = 3$; (b) For, $\alpha = 2$, $\beta = 2$ and $\gamma = 3$; (c) For, $\alpha = 2.5$, $\beta = 2$ and $\gamma = 3$; (d) For, $\alpha = 3$, $\beta = 2$ and $\gamma = 3$; (e) For, $\alpha = 3.5$, $\beta = 2$ and $\gamma = 3$.

Further it has been shown that $H_{\alpha,\beta,\gamma}(A)$ is a concave function obtaining its maximum value at $\mu_A(x_i) = \frac{1}{2}$. Hence $H_{\alpha,\beta,\gamma}(A)$ is increasing function of $\mu_A(x_i)$ in interval [0, 0.5) and decreasing function of $\mu_A(x_i)$ in interval (0.5, 1].

5. Conclusions

In this chapter, after reviewing some literatures on measures of information for fuzzy sets, a new generalised fuzzy information measure involving two parameters α and β has been introduced.

The necessary properties of the proposed measure have been verified and further it has been studied that the proposed measure is a concave function as it has shown monotonicity.

Further, a new generalised fuzzy information measure involving three parameters α, β and γ has been suggested and their necessary and required properties are examined. Thereafter, its validity is also verified. Also, the monotonic behaviour of fuzzy information measure of order α, β and γ has been conferred.

Fuzzy sets are indispensable in fuzzy system model and fuzzy system design, while the measurement of fuzziness in fuzzy sets is the fuzzy entropy or fuzzy information measure. Therefore, fuzzy information measures occupy important place in the processing of system design. Thus there are enormous applications of fuzzy information in the design of neural network classifiers.

Conflict of interest

I declare that I have no conflict of interest.

Author details

Anjali Munde

Address all correspondence to: anjalidhiman2006@gmail.com

Amity University, Uttar Pradesh, India

References

[1] Shannon C. A mathematical theory of communication. Bell System Technical Journal. 1948;**379–423**:623-659

[2] Zadeh L. Fuzzy sets. Information and Control. 1966;**8**:94-102

[3] Renyi A. On measures of entropy and information. In: Proceedings of the 4th Berkeley Symposium on Mathematical Statistics and Probability; University of California Press; 1961. pp. 547-561

[4] Havrada J, Charvat F. Quantification methods of classification processes: Concept of structural α-entropy. Kybernetika. 1967;**3**:30-31

[5] Behara M, Chawla J. Generalized γ-entropy. Selecta Statistica Canadiana. 1974;**2**:15-38

[6] Kapur J. A comparative assessment of various measures of directed divergence. Advances in Management Studies. 1984;**3**:1-16

[7] Kapur J. Measures of Fuzzy Information. New Delhi: Mathematical Sciences Trust Society; 1997

[8] Kaufmann A. Fuzzy Subsets Fundamental Theoretical Elements. New York: Academic Press; 1980

[9] De Luca A, Termini S. A definition of a non-probabilistic entropy in setting of fuzzy sets. Information and Control. 1972;**20**:301-312

[10] Bhandari D, Pal N. Some new information measures for fuzzy sets. Information Sciences. 1993;**67**:209-228

[11] Sharma B, Taneja I. Entropies of type (α, β) and other generalized measures of information theory. Metrika. 1975;**22**:202-215

[12] Kapur J. Measures of Information and their Applications. New York: Wiley Eastern; 1995

[13] Kosko B. Fuzzy entropy and conditioning. Information Sciences. 1986;**40**:165-174

[14] Pal N, Pal S. Object background segmentation using new definition of entropy. IEEE Proceedings. 1989;**136**(A):284-295

[15] Prakash O, Gandhi C. New measures of information based upon measures of central tendency and dispersion. International Review of Pure and Applied Mathematics. 2008;**4**: 161-172

[16] Prakash O, Gandhi C. New generalized measures of fuzzy entropy and their properties. Journal of Informatics and Mathematical Sciences. 2011;**3**:1-9

[17] Parkash O, Singh R. On characterization of useful information theoretic measures. Kybernetika. 1987;**23**:245-251

[18] Taneja I. On generalized information measures and their applications. Advances in Electronics and Electron Physics. 1989;**76**:327-413

[19] Taneja H, Tuteja R. Characterization of quantitative-qualitative measure of relative information. Information Sciences. 1984;**33**:217-222

[20] Tuteja R. On characterization of nonadditive measures of relative information and inaccuracy. Bulletin of the Calcutta Mathematical Society. 1983;**77**:363-369

[21] Tuteja R, Hooda D. On a generalized useful information measure of type α and degree β. Journal of the Indian Society of Statistics and Operations Research. 1985;**6**:1-11

[22] Tuteja R, Jain P. Characterization of relative useful information having utilities as monotone functions. Aplikace Matematiky. 1986;**31**:10-18

[23] Tuteja R, Jain P. An axiomatic characterization of relative useful information. Journal of Information and Optimization Sciences. 1986;**7**:49-57

[24] Tahayori H, Livi L, Sadeghian A, Rizzi A. Interval type-2 fuzzy set reconstruction based on fuzzy information-theoretic kernels. IEEE Transactions on Fuzzy Systems. 2015;**23**(4): 1014-1029

[25] Kumar T, Bajaj R. NTV metric based entropies of interval-valued intuitionistic fuzzy sets and their applications in decision making. Ann. Fuzzy Math. Inform. 2015;**9**(1):1-21

[26] Mishra A, Hooda D, Jain D. On exponential fuzzy measures of information and discrimination. International Journal of Computer Applications. 2015;**119**(23):1-7

[27] Hooda D, Mishra A. On trigonometric fuzzy information measures. ARPN Journal of Science and Technology. 2015;**5**(3):145-152

Optimization Methods Used in Fuzzy Logic

Development of a Genetic Fuzzy Controller and Its Application to a Noisy Inverted Double Pendulum

Anoop Sathyan and Kelly Cohen

Additional information is available at the end of the chapter

http://dx.doi.org/10.5772/intechopen.78786

Abstract

Fuzzy logic is used in a variety of applications due to its universal approximator attribute and non-linear characteristics. The tuning of the parameters of a fuzzy logic system, viz. the membership functions and the rulebase, requires a lot of trial and error. This process could be simplified by using a heuristic search algorithm like genetic algorithm (GA). In this chapter, we discuss the design of such a genetic fuzzy controller that can control an inverted double pendulum. GA improves the fuzzy logic controller (FLC) with each generation during the training process to obtain an FLC that can bring the pendulum to its inverted position. After training, the effectiveness of the FLC is tested for different scenarios by varying the initial conditions. We also show the effectiveness of the FLC even when subjected to noise and how the performance improves when the controller is tuned with noise.

Keywords: inverted double pendulum, genetic fuzzy control, fuzzy logic, machine learning, self-learning controllers

1. Introduction

Intelligent control techniques are gaining traction and increased focus and are being used in a wide variety of engineering applications. Fuzzy logic control is one such intelligent non-linear control technique that provides significant benefits in terms of design flexibility, universal approximator attribute and the ability to couple with optimization algorithms such as genetic algorithm (GA) for tuning its parameters. When coupled with the ability to capture expert or heuristic knowledge, and the ability to tune behavior in local envelopes of the operating space, fuzzy logic can be an indispensable control design tool in many applications. Fuzzy logic control also possesses inherent robustness due to having knowledge-based properties, making them good candidates for stochastic systems. One of the main challenges facing fuzzy logic control designers is the tuning of the membership functions and the heuristics involved. GA is used in this study to provide an autonomous guided search of the design space to develop a more optimized solution in accordance with the design requirements.

2. Literature review

Double pendulum is an example of a dynamic system that exhibits chaotic behavior. The inverted double pendulum is an archetype for thrust vector controlled multi-staged rocket or missile or even multi-rotor UAV flight control. The problem of controlling an inverted double pendulum has been studied for decades using different types of controllers. One of the approaches that has been used is a self-tuned neuro-PID controller to control the inverted pendulum on a cart [1]. The controller was realized by summing up two controllers for position and angle controls. They proved the effectiveness and robustness of this technique. An angular momentum based controller was able to control the double pendulum at any unstable position [2].

With the increase in computational capability and the advent of new and improved machine learning algorithms over the last decade, there has been an increase in the development of intelligent systems for various engineering applications such as path planning, target tracking, satellite attitude control systems [3], collaborative control of a swarm of UAVs [4], etc. Such intelligent systems provide various advantages, a few of which include adaptability, robustness to uncertainties and improved efficiency.

Fuzzy logic is one such intelligent system that can provide robustness and adaptability to controllers. Fuzzy logic was used in combination with optimal control theory to design a highly effective controller [5]. In a related research [6], fuzzy logic was used for stabilizing a parallel type double inverted pendulum. This is different from the inverted double pendulum in that it involves two separate pendulums being controlled simultaneously on a cart. Simulation results showed that the controller was able to stabilize completely the parallel-type double inverted pendulum system within 10s for a wide range of the initial angles of the two pendulums. The performance of fuzzy logic was compared to a PID controller in controlling an inverted pendulum [7]. Simulation results showed that the fuzzy logic controllers (FLCs) are far superior compared to PID controllers in terms of overshoot, settling time and response to parameter changes.

The performance of fuzzy controller tuned with noisy data was compared to that of a controller tuned without noise [8]. Optimizing the fuzzy system for a higher noise level results in good performance at lower noise levels. Lee presented three fuzzy system architectures and methods for automatically designing them for high dimensional problems [9]. The results indicate that the real coded algorithms consistently outperformed the binary coded algorithms in both the final performance of the system and the performance of the search algorithm. The Asymmetric-Triangular fuzzy systems consistently improved faster than the hyper-ellipsoidal and shared triangular representations in all cases.

Designing an FLS includes tuning the membership functions and the rulebase. This process can be automated by coupling GA with FLS to obtain the methodology known as Genetic

Fuzzy System (GFS). In a GFS, GA tunes the parameters of the FLS to minimize a cost function that is carefully chosen such that minimizing it provides the desired behavior of the system. Such GFSs have been developed with much success for clustering and task planning [10], aircraft conflict resolution [11], simulated air-to-air combat [12], collaborative control of UAVs, etc. Since fuzzy logic systems are made up of a set of membership functions that define the inputs and a set of linguistic rules that define the relationship between the inputs and the outputs, it is more interpretable compared to other machine learning techniques like neural networks and support vector machines. Since it is trained using GA, differentiable cost functions such as integral squared error is not required. So, as long as the mission requirement can be defined as a mathematical cost function, we do not need to have ground truth data available. GA will traverse the search space looking for the optimal set of membership functions and rulebase that minimizes the cost function, which makes it a form of reinforcement learning. Reinforcement learning is a branch of machine learning where an agent is trained to take the optimal control action to maximize a reward.

3. Problem formulation

The objective is to design two fuzzy logic controllers that control the torques at the two joints to bring the double pendulum to its inverted position from any initial condition as shown in **Figure 1**. T_1 and T_2 are the torques applied by the controller at the joints. GA is used to tune the fuzzy membership functions as well as the rule base to come up with the best possible solution, which settles at $\theta_1 = 0$, $\theta_2 = 0$, in minimum time. The position of the masses m_1 and m_2 are given by

$$x_1 = l_1 \sin \theta_1 \tag{1}$$

$$y_1 = l_1 \cos \theta_1 \tag{2}$$

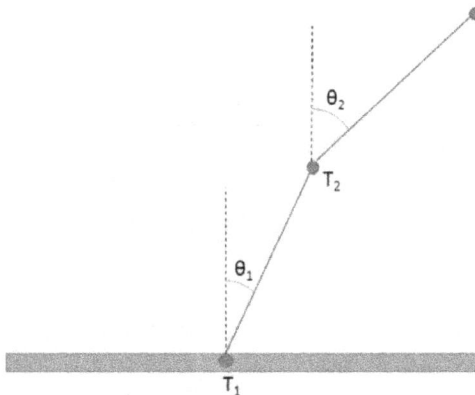

Figure 1. Double pendulum schematic with controllers at the joints.

$$x_2 = l_1 \sin\theta_1 + l_2 \sin\theta_2 \tag{3}$$

$$y_2 = l_1 \cos\theta_1 + l_2 \cos\theta_2 \tag{4}$$

The equations of motion of the double pendulum when torques T_1 and T_2 act at the joints are given below.

$$T_1 + (m_1 + m_2) L_1^2 \ddot{\theta}_1 + m_2 L_1 L_2 \ddot{\theta}_2 \cos(\theta_1 - \theta_2) + m_2 L_1 L_2 \dot{\theta}_2^2 \sin(\theta_1 - \theta_2)$$
$$+(m_1 + m_2) g L_1 \sin\theta_1 = 0 \tag{5}$$

$$T_2 + m_2 L_2^2 \ddot{\theta}_2 + m_2 L_1 L_2 \ddot{\theta}_1 \cos(\theta_1 - \theta_2) - m_2 L_1 L_2 \dot{\theta}_1^2 \sin(\theta_1 - \theta_2)$$
$$+m_2 g L_2 \sin\theta_2 = 0 \tag{6}$$

Assumptions

1. The masses m_1 and m_2 are assumed to be concentrated at the joints.

2. The masses m_1 and m_2 are considered as particles.

3. The rods are assumed to be massless.

4. Non-conservative forces like friction, air resistance, etc., are not considered.

5. There is no delay in the transmission of torque from the controller to the joint.

6. The motion is constrained to two dimensions. Hence $z = 0$.

7. The rods do not undergo expansion or compression. Thus, Eqs. (1)–(4) are satisfied.

4. Methodology

The flow chart showing the process of genetic fuzzy logic design as applied to the case of the inverted double pendulum is shown in **Figure 2**. Fuzzy logic is used to determine the torques acting on the two joints, T_1 and T_2. In order to reduce the computational complexity, each of the inputs and outputs are defined by just three membership functions as shown in **Figure 3**.

GA is used to tune a 15-element vector R. GA is a search heuristic inspired from the process of natural selection that can perform an extensive search of a complicated n-D space, where n is the number of variables, to find a near optimal solution. For this research, $n = 15$. GA starts off with an initial set of random solutions also called a population of individuals, the size of which is pre-defined. There are two main operators in GA viz., crossover and mutation.

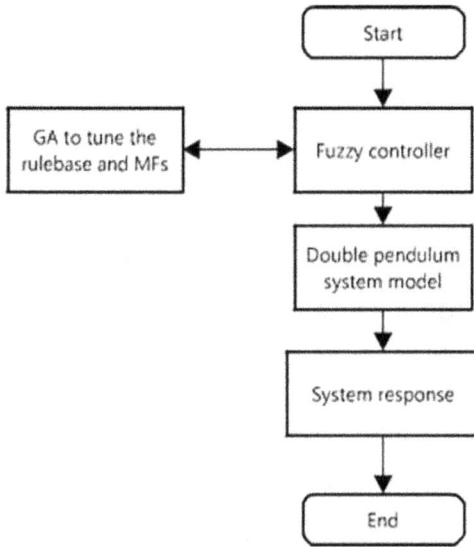

Figure 2. Flowchart showing the genetic fuzzy logic methodology used for designing controllers for the inverted double pendulum problem [13].

The crossover requires two individuals and some portion of the two solution vectors are interchanged to obtain two child individuals. In a mutation, some values in a chosen individual are arbitrarily changed to obtain a new individual. The cost functions of all the resulting individuals are evaluated and the ones with lower cost values have higher probability of moving onto the next generation.

The first 9 elements in the vector, $R(1-9)$, represent the rules as shown in **Table 1** and $R(10-15)$ represent the boundaries of the membership functions as shown in **Figure 3**. The membership functions are assumed to be symmetric around zero. $R(1-9)$ are integers with values from one to three. One, two and three represent negative (N), zero (ZO) and positive (P) membership functions for the inputs, respectively.

For this research, we use centroid defuzzification to obtain the crisp output values. The rulebase is assumed to be same for both the controllers T1 and T2. AND operator connects the inputs θ and $\dot{\theta}$. For example,

$\dot{\theta}$	N	ZO	P
θ			
N	R(1)	R(2)	R(3)
ZO	R(4)	R(5)	R(6)
P	R(7)	R(8)	R(9)

Table 1. GA string values assigned to the rulebase during training.

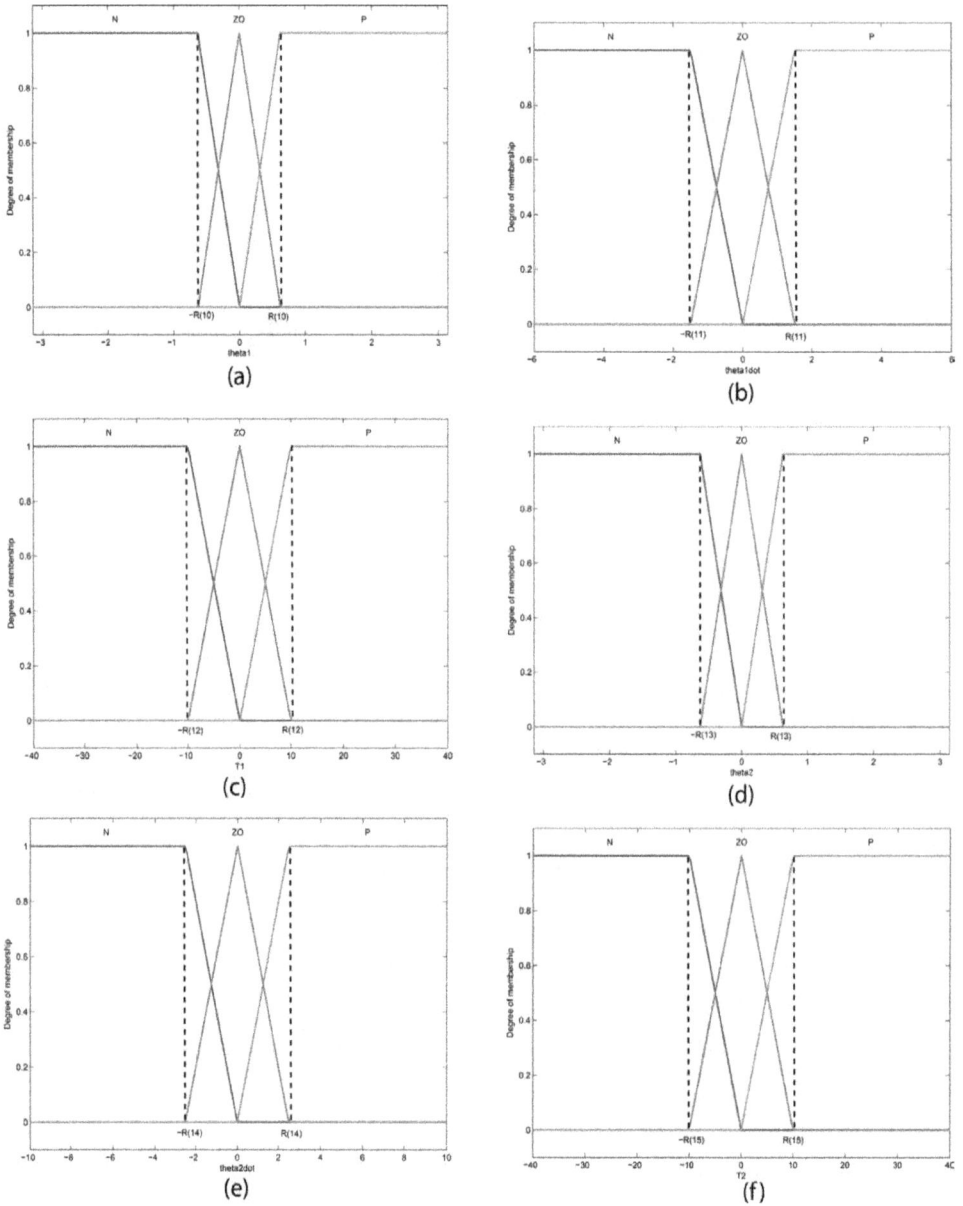

Figure 3. GA string values assigned to the input and output membership function boundaries for FIS1 [13].

$$If\ \theta_1\ is\ N\ AND\ \ is\ P,\ then\ T1\ is\ R(3).$$

The cost function that needs to be minimized by GA is given in Eq. (7). Since the cost function is an integral over time, it ensures that the system settles to the inverted position quickly. In our simulations, the simulation is performed for 5 s and hence $T = 5$.

$$f = \int_0^T \left(\theta_1^2 + \theta_2^2 + \dot{\theta}_1^2 + \dot{\theta}_2^2 \right) dt \qquad (7)$$

5. Numerical results and discussion

The system response is simulated for the following parameter values:

$$m_1 = 0.1kg$$

$$m_2 = 0.1kg$$

$$l_1 = 1m$$

$$l_2 = 1m$$

The FISs are tuned for 2 cases: (1) Without noise and (2) With 5% measurement noise applied to the inputs.

5.1. FIS tuned without noise

The rulebase obtained after tuning is shown in **Table 2**. The membership function boundaries are obtained as $R(10,15) = [0.5642\ 8.3738\ 7.1121\ 1.0264\ 4.2160\ 3.1641]$.

5.1.1. With zero initial angular velocity

The system response, with zero initial angular velocity, is shown in **Figure 4**. The system was tested for different starting positions and in each case, the response settles within 5 s. Settling time is the time it takes the response to settle within an absolute value of 0.01 rad. The genetic fuzzy controller works well even when it is subjected to noise in the angle measurements. The responses for 5 and 10% noise are shown in **Figure 5**. For the 5% noise scenario shown in **Figure 5(a)**, the controller brings the system to settle in a very smooth manner. Both θ_1 and θ_2 settle within 5 s. In the case of 10% noise shown in **Figure 5(b)**, θ_1 settles within 5 s, but θ_2 takes close to 10 s to settle. The response for θ_2 also shows a slight oscillation before settling down.

$\dot{\theta}$	N	ZO	P
θ			
N	P	P	ZO
ZO	P	ZO	N
P	ZO	N	N

Table 2. Rulebase obtained after training [13].

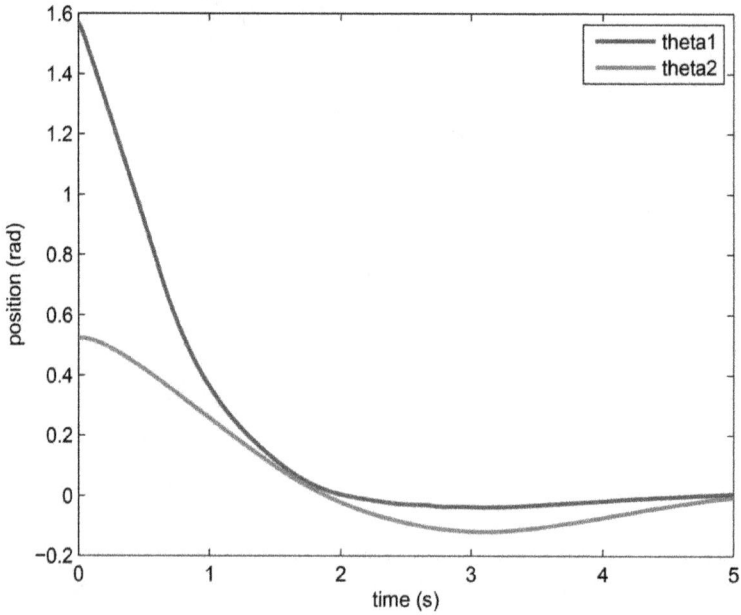

Figure 4. Controllers trained without noise: Plots showing $\theta_1(t)$ and $\theta_2(t)$ under no noise with zero initial angular velocities [13].

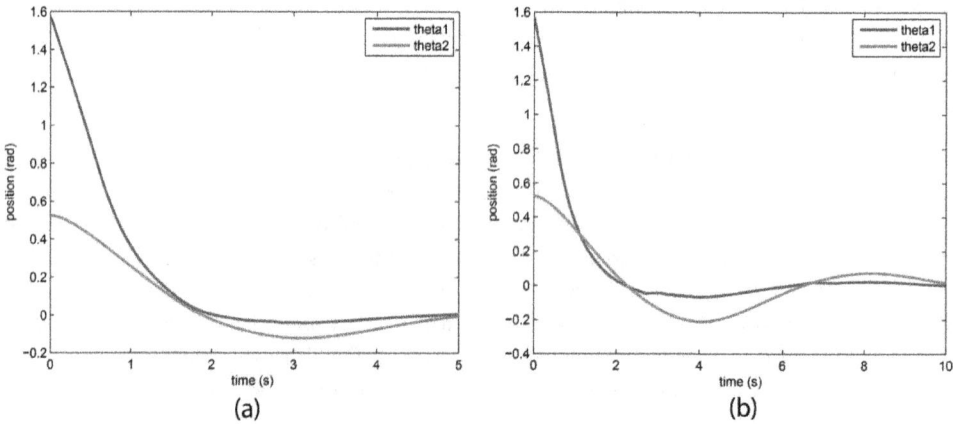

Figure 5. Controllers trained without noise: Plots showing $\theta_1(t)$ and $\theta_2(t)$ under (a) 5% noise and (b) 10% noise with zero initial angular velocities [13].

5.1.2. With non-zero initial angular velocities

In this case, initial angular velocities of 2 rad/s are considered ($\dot{\theta}_1 = 2\ rad/s, \dot{\theta}_2 = 2\ rad/s$). The system response is shown in **Figure 6**. The system was tested for different starting positions and in each case, the response settles within 10 s. Just like the previous case with no initial angular velocity, the

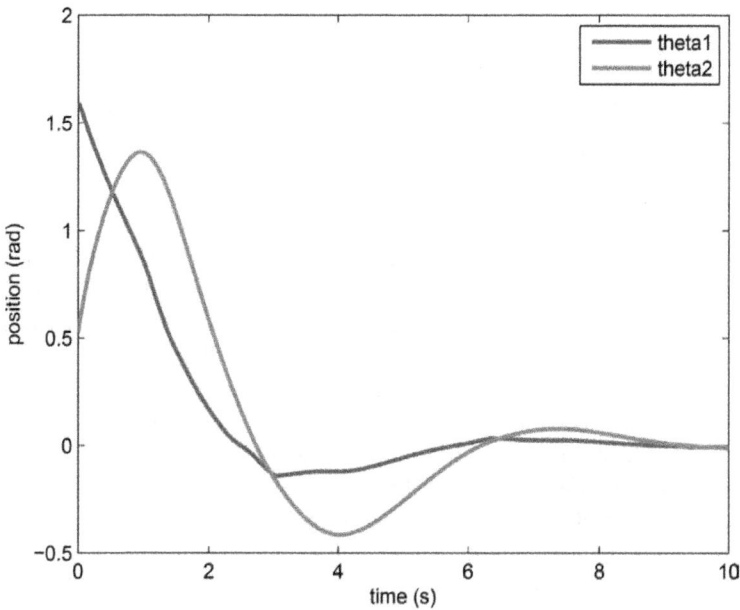

Figure 6. Controllers trained without noise: Plots showing $\theta_1(t)$ and $\theta_2(t)$ under no noise with initial angular velocities of 2 rad/s [13].

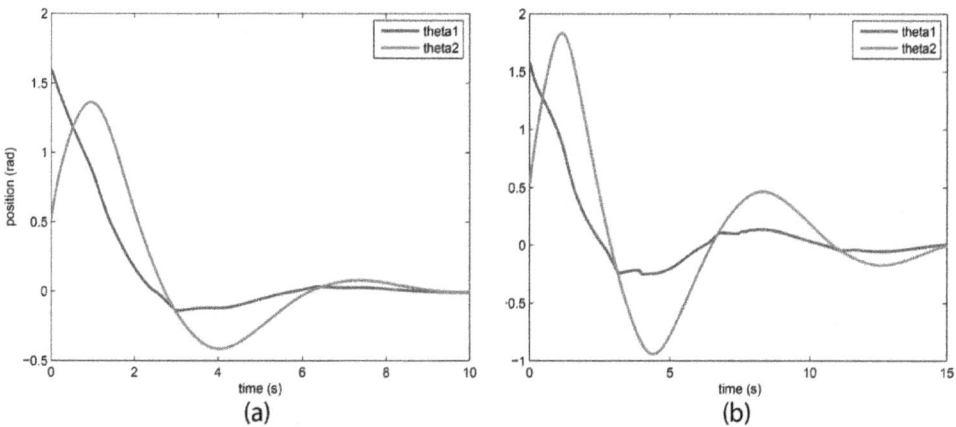

Figure 7. Controllers trained without noise: Plots showing $\theta_1(t)$ and $\theta_2(t)$ under (a) 5% noise and (b) 10% noise with initial angular velocities of 2 rad/s [13].

genetic fuzzy controller works well even when it is subjected to noise in the angle measurements. The responses for 5 and 10% noise are shown in **Figure 7**. For the 5% noise scenario shown in **Figure 7(a)**, the controller brings the system to settle within 10 s. Some oscillation can be observed, although insignificant. In the case of 10% noise shown in **Figure 7(b)**, θ_1 settles within 10 s, but θ_2 takes close to 15 s to settle. There is significant oscillation before it settles to $\theta_1 = 0$; $\theta_2 = 0$.

5.2. FIS tuned with 5% noise

In this case, the FIS is tuned with 5% noise and the response of the resulting controller is examined. The rulebase obtained is same as the one shown in **Table 2**. The membership function boundaries are obtained as $R(10:15) = [0.3100\ 11.9261\ 7.4158\ 0.8904\ 3.8477\ 3.5883]$.

5.2.1. With no initial angular velocity

The system response, with zero initial angular velocity, is shown in **Figure 8**. The system was tested for different starting positions and in each case, the response settles within 5 s. The genetic fuzzy controller works well even when it is subjected to noise in the angle measurements. The responses for 5 and 10% noise are shown in **Figure 9**. The controller is able to bring the system to settle within 5 s even in the presence of noise. Although there is a small undershoot, θ_1 settles much faster compared to the responses shown in **Figures 4** and **5**. There are no significant oscillations in the system response. It can be observed from **Figures 8** and **9** that the noise has a minuscule effect on the system response thus proving that the controller is very robust. Thus, when there is no initial angular velocity, the controller tuned for 5% noise performs much better, as expected.

5.2.2. With non-zero initial angular velocities

In this case, initial angular velocities of 2 rad/s are considered ($\dot{\theta}_1 = 2\ rad/s, \dot{\theta}_2 = 2\ rad/s$). The system response is shown in **Figure 10**. The system was tested for different starting positions

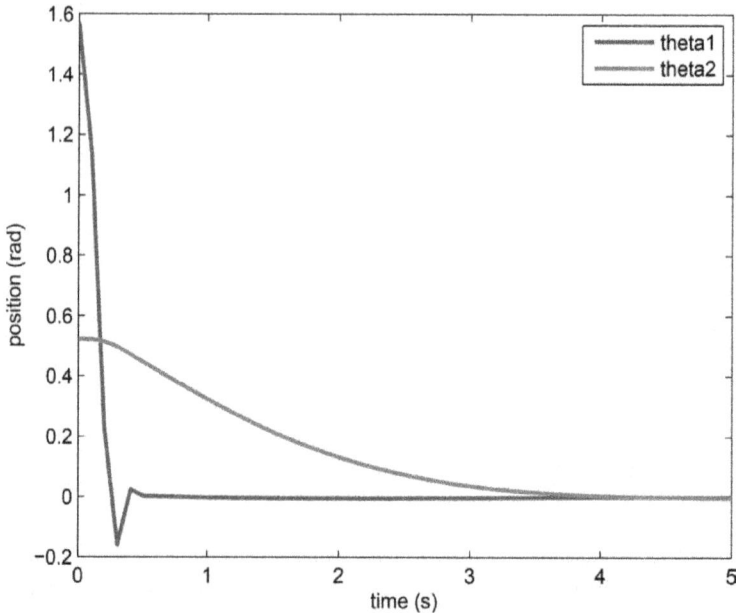

Figure 8. Controllers trained with 5% noise: plots showing $\theta_1(t)$ and $\theta_2(t)$ under no noise with zero initial angular velocities [13].

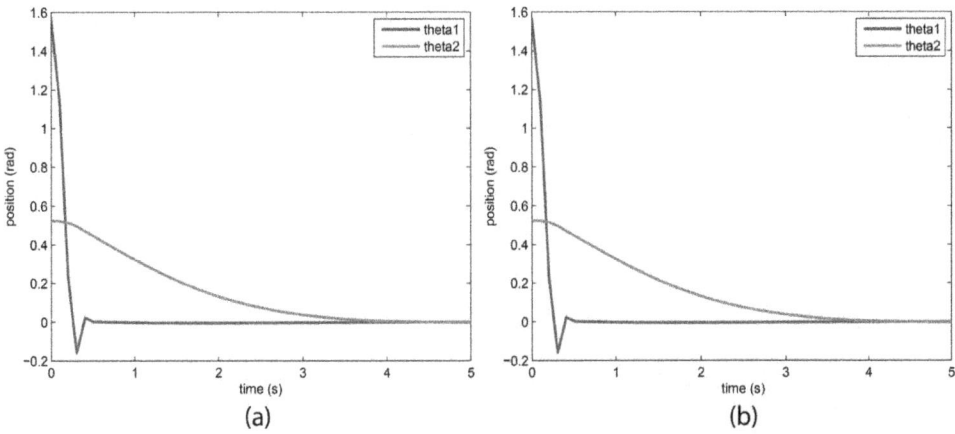

Figure 9. Controllers trained with 5% noise: plots showing $\theta_1(t)$ and $\theta_2(t)$ under (a) 5% noise and (b) 10% noise with zero initial angular velocities [13].

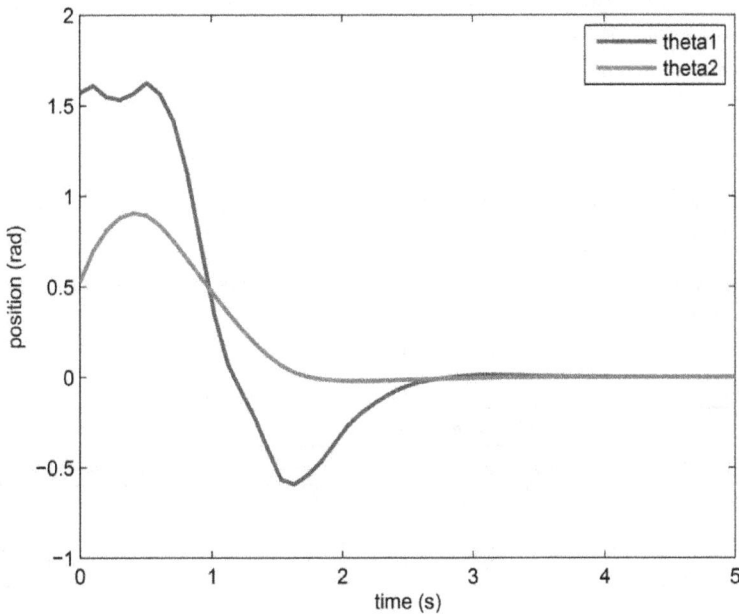

Figure 10. Controllers trained with 5% noise: plots showing $\theta_1(t)$ and $\theta_2(t)$ under no noise with initial angular velocities of 2 rad/s [13].

and in each case, the response settles within 5 s. The response of the controller when subjected to 5 and 10% noise are shown in **Figure 11**. For both cases, the controller brings the system to settle within 5 s. Even in the case of non-zero initial angular velocity, the controller is very resilient to noise. The settling time is less compared to the controller tuned without noise.

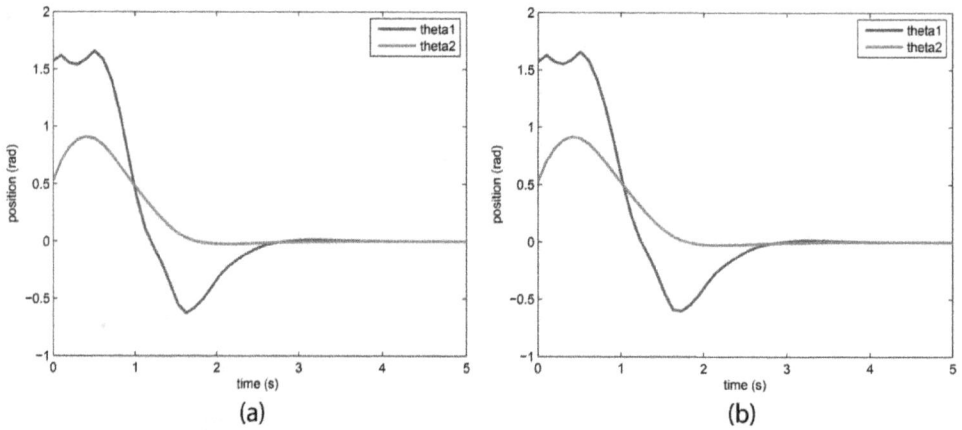

(a)   (b)

Figure 11. Controllers trained with 5% noise: plots showing $\theta_1(t)$ and $\theta_2(t)$ under (a) 5% noise and (b) 10% noise with initial angular velocities of 2 rad/s [13].

Table 3 compiles the results obtained for the double pendulum system. The table compares the settling time and the integral square error (ISE) for the two different controllers. The ISE is given by,

$$ISE = \int_0^\infty e^2(t)dt \tag{8}$$

where e(t) is the error obtained by subtracting the actual response and the desired response which in our case is zero.

It can be seen from **Table 3** that the settling time and ISE are better in the case of the controller tuned with 5% noise. Optimizing the controller with 5% noise helps with the system response for larger window of uncertainty. As can be seen from **Table 3**, the ISE values for 10% noise

		Controllers trained without noise			Controllers trained with 5% noise		
		No noise	5% Noise	10% Noise	No noise	5% Noise	10% Noise
$\dot{\theta}_1 = \dot{\theta}_2 = 0$	$Ts(\theta_1)$	1.632	1.636	1.708	0.3895	0.3906	0.3911
	$Ts(\theta_2)$	3.871	3.874	5.723	2.1532	2.1545	2.1560
	$ISE(\theta_1)$	0.8825	0.8853	0.8961	0.3875	0.3943	0.4012
	$ISE(\theta_2)$	0.2412	0.2450	0.3323	0.0985	0.0988	0.0990
$\dot{\theta}_1 = \dot{\theta}_2 = 2$	$Ts(\theta_1)$	4.431	4.487	5.191	2.347	2.368	2.449
	$Ts(\theta_2)$	5.208	5.271	13.538	1.475	1.487	1.531
	$ISE(\theta_1)$	3.4389	3.5963	5.9624	2.2963	2.3440	2.4009
	$ISE(\theta_2)$	3.2142	3.4433	11.0016	0.6271	0.6363	0.6674

Table 3. Comparison of settling times (Ts in seconds) and the ISE for the scenarios discussed before [13].

scenario in the case of the controller tuned without noise is on the higher side. But, this gets reduced when the controller is tuned for 5% noise. Thus, the overall performance of the system increases by tuning the controller with 5% measurement noise.

6. Conclusions

This chapter discussed the design of genetic fuzzy controllers to control an inverted double pendulum. While fuzzy logic by itself works well, tuning the parameters involved to satisfy a specific requirement might need a lot of trial and error to be done by the researchers. Incorporating GA to tune these parameters solves this problem. In this chapter, the objective was to bring the system to its inverted position. The time-integral cost function ensured that the FISs are trained to reduce the settling time.

The genetic fuzzy controller was able to stabilize the double pendulum at the inverted position starting from any initial position. The controller was tuned for two cases: (1) when there is no noise, and (2) when subjected to 5% noise. For each of the two cases, the results were shown for two sub-cases: (a) with zero initial angular velocities and (b) with non-zero initial angular velocities. The controller tuned for 5% has a better performance than the one tuned without noise. Tuning the controller with 5% noise improves the robustness of the system for a larger window of uncertainty. Since a lot of real-life systems suffer from measurement noise, it is important to develop robust controllers that can make decisions even when the inputs are noisy.

Author details

Anoop Sathyan* and Kelly Cohen

*Address all correspondence to: sathyaap@ucmail.uc.edu

Department of Aerospace Engineering and Engineering Mechanics, University of Cincinnati, USA

References

[1] Omatu S, Fujinaka T, Yoshioka M. Neuro-PID control for inverted single and double pendulums. In: IEEE International Conference on Systems, Man and Cybernetics; 2000

[2] Azad M, Featherstone R. Angular momentum based controller for balancing an inverted double pendulum, Romansy 19–robot design, Dynamics and Control. Vienna: Springer; 2013. pp. 251-258

[3] Walker A, Putman P, Cohen K. Fuzzy logic attitude control of a magnetically actuated CubeSat. In: AIAA Infotech@ Aerospace (I@ A) Conference; 2013

[4]   Ernest N, Cohen K, Schumacher C. UAV swarm routing through genetic fuzzy learning methods. In: AIAA Infotech@ Aerospace Conference; Boston; 2013

[5]   Cheng F, Zhong G, Li Y, Xu Z. Fuzzy control of a double-inverted pendulum. Fuzzy Sets and Systems. 1996;**79**(3):315-321

[6]   Yi J, Yubazaki N, Hirota K. A new fuzzy controller for stabilization of parallel-type double inverted pendulum system. Fuzzy Sets and Systems. 2002;**126**(1):105-119

[7]   Li-ping Y, Pei-jin W. Study on PID Control of a Single Inverted Pendulum System. Beijing, China: Control Engineering of China; 2007

[8]   Pawar P, Ganguli R. Structural Health Monitoring Using Genetic Fuzzy Systems. London, England: Springer Science & Business Media; 2011. Chapter 3

[9]   Lee M. On genetic representation of high dimensional fuzzy systems. In: Uncertainty Modeling and Analysis; and Annual Conference of the North American Fuzzy Information Processing Society; 1995

[10] Sathyan A, Ernest N, Cohen K. An efficient genetic fuzzy approach to UAV swarm routing. Unmanned Systems. 2016;**4**(02):117-127

[11] Sathyan A, Ernest N, Lavigne L, Cazaurang F, Kumar M, Cohen K. A Genetic Fuzzy Logic Based Approach to Solving the Aircraft Conflict Resolution Problem. Grapevine, TX: AIAA Information Systems-AIAA Infotech@ Aerospace; 2017

[12] Ernest N, Carroll D, Schumacher C, Clark M, Cohen K, Lee G. Genetic fuzzy based artificial intelligence for unmanned combat aerial vehicle control in simulated air combat missions. Journal of Defense Management. 2016;**6**(144):2167-0374

[13] Sathyan A. Intelligent machine learning approaches for aerospace applications [Doctoral dissertation]. University of Cincinnati; 2017

Application of Fuzzy Logic in Various Research Fields

Chapter 4

Fuzzy Logic Applications in Metrology Processes

Bloul Benattia

Additional information is available at the end of the chapter

http://dx.doi.org/10.5772/intechopen.79381

Abstract

Three-dimensional metrology is concerned with checking the conformity of machined parts with the geometrical specifications on their definition drawings from the design office. Three-dimensional measurement is a firmly established technique in the industry. For this, we apply the fuzzy logic to solve probing. Probing technology is widely used in three-dimensional metrology. In addition, we measure the very small dimensions, that is, the measurement at the micrometer scales. This chapter presents a new approach to the developing gear curve (CMMs). This method aims to select the most likely contact point for each successive arc by applying geometrical criteria and a fuzzy logic estimator, as you know there are several methods, but the fuzzy logic is more efficient and closer to the profile reel. The fuzzy logic system is particularly suitable for application to the three-dimensional metrology, including applications on a small radius probe as well as probing discontinuities to the flank profile. In addition, the time allowed is 144.09 s. Tests were carried out on gearboxes of agricultural machinery in the factory of my country (Algerian Tractors Company).

Keywords: metrology, fuzzy logic, gears, model gears, probe, path

1. Introduction

Coordinate measuring machines (CMMs) are becoming increasingly important in measurements and the verification of the dimensional quality of manufactured parts and products. First, today's gear inspection is a description of the nominal geometry of the gear teeth, which are limited some flank profile traces. The new principle of the corrected determination of the measured point in the metrology of coordinates is brought to the system of the fuzzy logic. This means that for the measurement with great accuracy of a complex surface's mechanical part, we propose a new algorithm for the compensation of the tip of the radius of the stylus in a process of scanning by three-dimensional coordinate CMMs. The proposed algorithm is dedicated to high-definition measurement. Advantages of the algorithm are that we do not calculate the normal vector and we do not use a Non-uniform rational basis spline (NURBS) is a mathematical model commonly used in computer graphics for generating and representing curves and surfaces. It offers great flexibility and precision for handling both analytic and modeled shapes. In general, editing NURBS curves and surfaces is highly intuitive and predictable. Control points are always either connected directly to the curve / surface, or act as if they were connected by a rubber band [1]. The method is based on the fuzzy logic algorithm, which is a well-known method to approximate the ideal position that minimizes the sum of the squared residual errors between the clearance and the model. This choice is motivated by the robustness of this method and it is important to underline here that no attempt to implement it within the coordinate measuring machine (CMMs) software has been reported in the three-dimensional metrology literature. Digital applications have dealt with the case of a gear tooth gear that is fitted to the gearbox of machine tools. The comparison between the real surface obtained by the three-dimensional measuring machine and the ideal model that gives us defects of shape of the tooth. But this precision is generally obtained only for the measurement of well-known shapes of the piece measured and when its dimensions greatly exceed the radius of the tip of the probe, and for this reason, the algorithm is used for the correction of the radius of the probe. For example, simple surfaces form profiles that are not geometric primitive sections known as planes (circle, sphere, cone, gear, etc.).

2. Fuzzy logic applications in metrology processes

Metrology engineering has employed fuzzy logic in the detection of the defect of gears with straight cylindrical teeth. It has also been applied to process control, the modeling of the developing profile of a tooth circle, its optimizations, looks for defects in shape, and position.

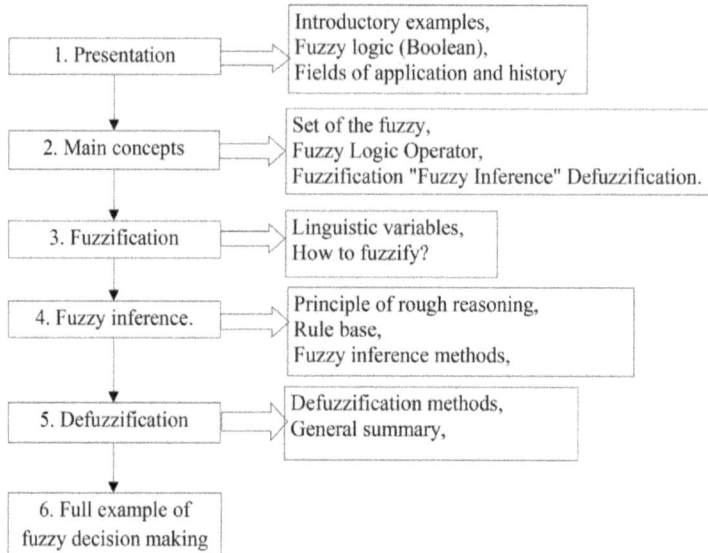

Figure 1. Synoptic of fuzzy logic.

In this research, we investigate these applications in more detail. See the synoptic of fuzzy logic in **Figure 1**.

3. Geometry and the specification of spur gear with the module

Pressure angle remains the same throughout the operation, and the teeth are weaker. It is easier to manufacture due to its convex surface. The velocity is not affected due to the variation in the central distance. Interference takes place; there is more wear and tear as contact takes place between convex surfaces (**Figure 2**).

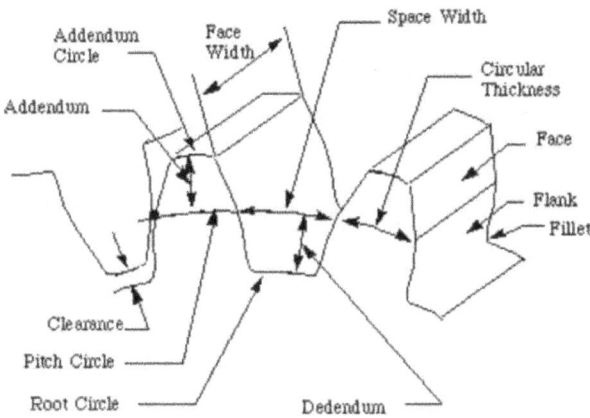

Figure 2. Involute profile.

4. The implementation of fuzzy logic systems

4.1. Problem of probing the tooth

Firstly, the probing obstacle is in zones 1 and 2 when the information is entered by the tridimensional measuring machine (see **Figure 3**). Indeed, we saw that the segment (ab) is undefined after having transferred the coordinates of the center of the ball. That is, there are no coordinates for probing this one (**Figure 3-1**), and the same goes for zone 2; when we did the transfer, no results were interpreted because the segment (ab) is unknown. To solve this problem of probing, we apply the system and notions of fuzzy logic.

4.2. The principle of determination of the measured point corrected

As regards the measurement with high accuracy on CMMs, we specify the probe path. For this, we propose a new algorithm for the compensation of the radius of the tip of the stylus in a process of scanning the surface of the tooth by CMMs. The proposed algorithm is dedicated to the measurement of high definition. It is done to calculate the normal vector.

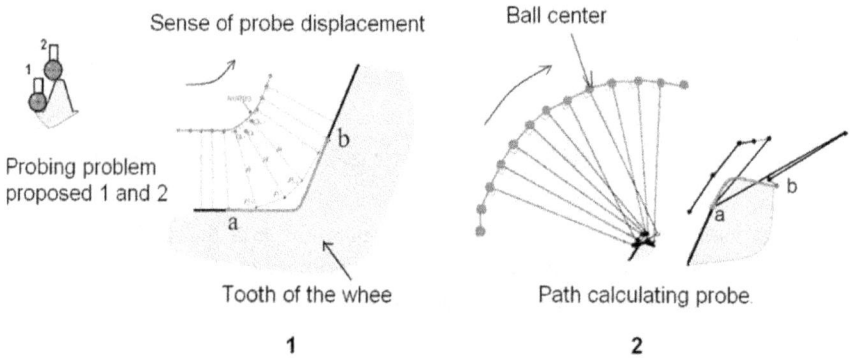

Figure 3. Problem of probing the tooth of a wheel.

The proposed compensation method consists of the following steps [1]:

- realization of a series of high-density measurements on the characteristic of geometry measured by the spherical stylus tip,

- contour of the sample defines a bow per ball, for each measured point,

- calculating the points of intersection A_i and A_{i+1} for each arc, with the next and the previous point,

- for each arc, the estimate of the point of contact with S_i as the characteristic of this point is located in the middle of the arc,

- determination of angular compensation using the fuzzy logic knowledge base and the application of compensation based on the corresponding angular adjustment.

The calculation of angles $\Delta\alpha_i$ can be achieved by exploiting a known basic variety or other-rule artificial intelligence techniques [2, 3]. In the experimental implementation of this method, we opted for the calculation of the angles $\Delta\alpha_i$ with a fuzzy logic algorithm [4].

4.3. Analysis of the geometry of the probe trajectory

We consider point O_i as one of the data points describing the position of the center of the ball of the spherical stylus registered by the CMMs (see **Figure 4**) [5]. We take the previous additional points O_{i-1} and the following point O_{i+1}. Considering the external envelope tip of the stylus at the O_i point, it can be said that the ball of the stylus is always in contact with the material of the gears and that no part can be at the limit of the tip of the stylus; the point of contact of the stylus ball with the measuring surface is on the arc A_iA_{i+1}. The points A_i and A_{i+1} have points of intersection of the three circles that have the centers O_i, O_{i-1} and O_{i+1}, respectively [6].

All three circles have a radius R equal to the radius of the stylus ball, with which the preliminary calculations of the CMMs are made, according to the qualification of the probe system. All points of the arc are selected to transfer the corrected measured points associated with the

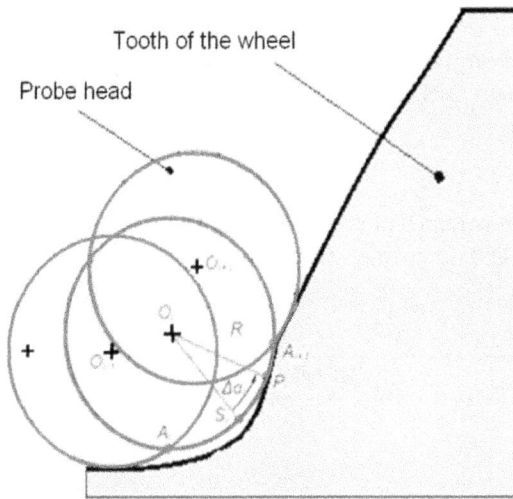

Figure 4. Analyzes the geometry of the sweep path for the determination of the measured point corrected.

measured points O_i. However, as a first approximation, the ideal points of the stylus ball in contact with the measuring surface are evaluated midway on the arc: A_iA_{i+1}. Indeed, some adjustments of the corrected measured point may be essential.

In the first estimate, a preliminary point S_i was chosen to the bow A_iA_{i+1}. Then, we take into account the mutual position of the neighboring points, O_i and $O_{i-m}, \dots, O_{i-1}$ and $O_{i+1}, \dots O_{i+n}$. (where m and n are a number of previous and following points, respectively). An angular adjustment $\Delta\alpha_i$ is obtained to improve the new position of the ideal point of contact with the flank and the ball and thus correctly calculate the points which are the closest P_i. Calculations of $\Delta\alpha_i$ can rely on artificial intelligence techniques that are based on the rules of fuzzy logic. In the experimental implementation, we use the method of correction the measurement of the points of stylus (stylus tip envelop method). We opted for a fuzzy logic algorithm to compute $\Delta\alpha_i$. The entry of this system of logic is summarized in **Table 2** with two components: $\Delta\alpha_i, Az_i$, and Δk_i. We define the first magnitude Δz_i which is the distance between point O_i and the point of intersection with the line $(O_{i-1}O_{i+1})$. The second component, Δk_i, is the distance between point O_i and the point of intersection with the line $(O_{i-1} O_{i-2})$. These elements define the input values and output (see **Figure 4**).

4.3.1. Inputs

The choice of input and output variables depends on the control we want to achieve and the available parameters. In our chapter, we can consider the entries x_m and y_m which are the Cartesian coordinates of the points entered by the three-dimensional measuring machine in the course of scanning the surface of the right or left flank by the probing system. This choice is intuitive and based on the experience of the operator.

4.3.2. Output

The outputs are based on the problem that was posed; anyway, we can find one or more outputs and so on. Finally, it is lucid that the outputs in our work are two: x_m and y_m.

4.3.3. Fuzzification

First, we proposed the parameters in our tests on the CMMs, which are within the Metrology Laboratory of ENP-Oran (see **Table 1**). These are very important for simulation calculations.

	Minimum value	Maximum value
t (s)	—	250
θ (radian)	0.2	30
x_m (mm)	—	26
y_m (mm)	—	26
i	100	200
Δk_i	—	200
Δz_i	—	200
α_i	—	200

Table 1. Parameters of the test.

So this step allowed us to give the different linguistic variables that will be used during the gear control by the fuzzy logic [7–15].

4.3.4. Rule base (inference)

Indeed, we exploit **Table 2** to build the inference of fuzzy logic in C; however, we do not have to complete all the boxes. The rules are developed by an expert and his knowledge of the problem [12, 13, 15].

$$IF\ conditions....THEN\ action$$

$$IF conditions...THEN\ action \tag{1}$$

4.4. Construction of fuzzy logic matrix

The matrix is in the form of **Table 2** or a matrix that we can build according to the previous parameters, Δk_i, $\Delta \alpha_i$, and Δz_i, while the purpose of this table is to know which elements are most influenced during the implementation of fuzzy logic to spur gears.

Table 2. Matrix of fuzzy logic.

N.B: After completing the logic matrix of **Table 2**, it was concluded that the factors that influenced on the logic estimator are:

$$Matrix = \begin{bmatrix} 0 & 0 & 0 & 0 & 0 \\ 0 & 1 & 0 & 0 & 0 \\ 0 & 0 & 1 & 0 & 0 \\ 0 & 0 & 0 & 1 & 0 \\ 0 & 0 & 0 & 0 & 0 \end{bmatrix} \qquad (2)$$

5. Probing and data processing

Over the last 20 years, remarkable progress has been made in three-dimensional measurement technology with regard to the mechanical elements of the machine, control equipment, and software.

6. Instruments for measuring capacity

The accuracy of the probe during scanning is generally several tens of micrometers, but this accuracy is generally not achieved for the measurement of well-known shapes as well as when the size of the part greatly exceeds the radius of the feeler ball because of the algorithms used for the sharp radius of correction stylets.

For example, spline profiles that do not compose a part of a geometric primitive known as (circle, sphere, cone, torus, etc.), they present particular difficulties to establish the method of the normal vector. Left surfaces are now very common (car, bodies, consumer products of ergonomic shapes, turbine blades, etc.).

In addition, small features become commonplace and, although measurements are made by digitization, the correction can result in the introduction of unacceptable errors [16–18].

7. Measures the coordinates of tooth profile points by the three-dimensional measuring machine (CMM)

In fact, this semi-experimental part is very important for applying these notions of fuzzy logic to the contour of the flank of the left or right tooth. However, we are able to bring back information through a known mathematical model or by asking a laboratory to provide it to us. In short, the result of the processing of information is the same, either by borrowing the mathematical model or by directly probing by CMM (see **Figures 4–6**) [8, 11].

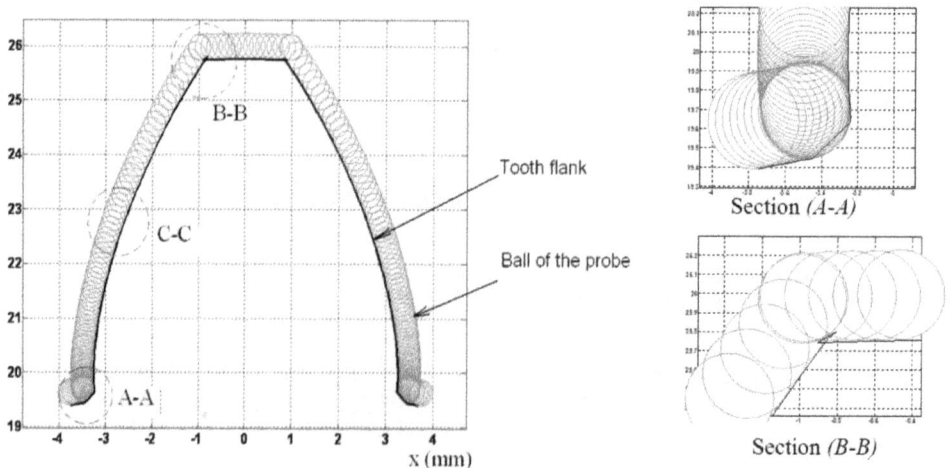

Figure 5. Mathematical model: sections (A-A), (B-B) and (C-C).

8. Presentation of the algorithm

The presentation of the fuzzy logic algorithm has been introduced (see **Figure 6**); this logic affects one or more steps of the algorithm to try to increase its performance including accuracy and speed, and there are several variables. Some of these variables expand, and the abbreviation of the corresponding iterative point asserts that it would be a good response to the algorithm. To make an algorithm choice, there are several criteria that must be checked:

- speed,
- precision,

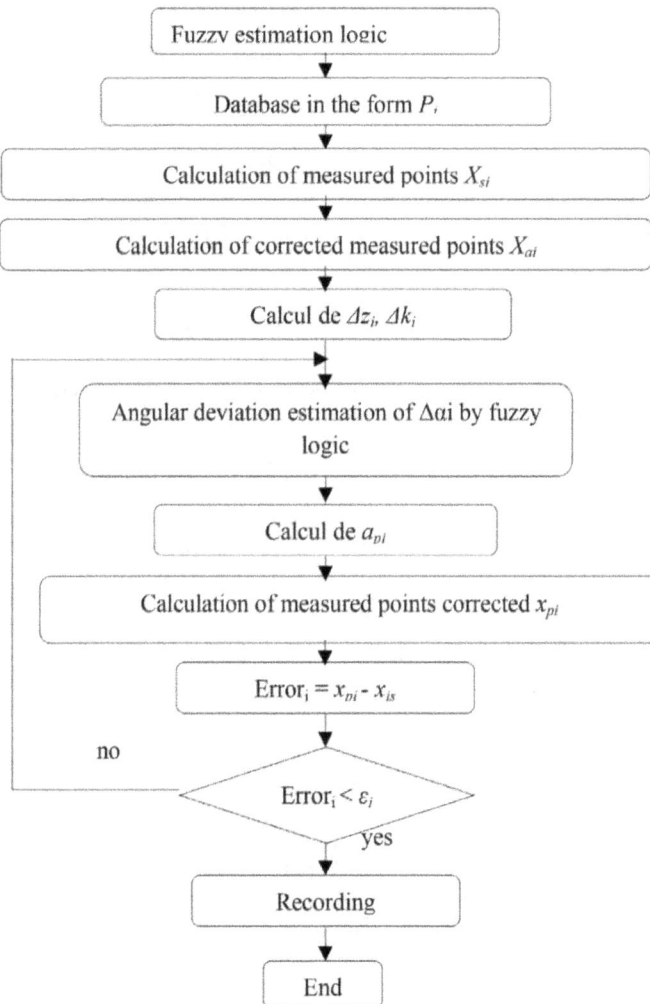

Figure 6. Flowchart of fuzzy estimator logic.

- stability,

- robustness and simplicity.

The importance of any of these four criteria depends on the application of the final program. The development of a complete system of the quality inspection of the manufactured parts requires the coordination of a set of processes to acquire data, its dimensional evaluations, and comparisons with the proposed reference model. For this, it is essential to make certain conceptual knowledge profitable not only for the object to be analyzed but also for the environment. In this case, the goal of this chapter is to establish a procedure for automating the modeling of the surface inspection of complex parts such as gears. Allowing to correct the relative differences of the manufacturing parameters, then, the adopted criteria includes fast convergence, the robustness of the system, and the simplicity of the interface. Finally, the new algorithm is summarized by the diagram of the following flowchart [2]:

9. Calculation of the corrected measured points

We used the following equations to achieve these results (see **Figure 7**). Equation of right which is between the points P_{i+1}, P_{i-1}:

$$y_i = a_i x_i + b_i \tag{3}$$

The equation of the line that passes through the point Pi and perpendicular to the line that passes through the points $(P_{i+1}P_{i-1})$:

$$y_i = c_i.x_i + d_i \tag{4}$$

The equation between two points P_{i-1}, P_{i-2}:

$$y_i = e_i x_i + f_i \tag{5}$$

The equation of the line that passes through the point P_i and perpendicular to the line $(P_{i-1}P_{i-2})$:

$$y_i = m_i x_i + n_i \tag{6}$$

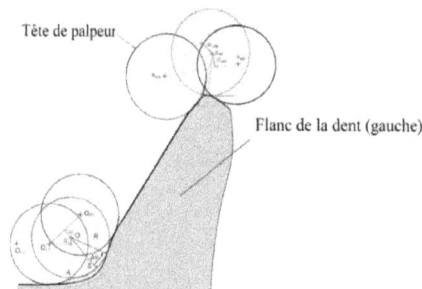

Figure 7. Determination of Ak_i, $\Delta\alpha_i$, Az_i (sections B-Band C-C).

We take theoretically the tolerance values for each point gained in the range (0.0001.rd).

Equation of the circle includes

$$(x - x_i)^2 + (y - y_i)^2 = r^2 \tag{7}$$

(see **Figure 7**)

r is the radius of the probe sphere (r = 0.2–5 mm).

We have determined the following values $a_i, b_i, c_i, d_i, \Delta_i$.

$$
\begin{cases}
a_i = \dfrac{y_{i+1} - y_{i-1}}{x_{i+1} - x_{i-1}} \\
b_i = y_{i-1} - \dfrac{y_{i+1} - y_{i-1}}{x_{i+1} - x_{i-1}} . x_{i-1} \\
c_i = -1/a_i \\
d_i = y_i - c_i . x_i \\
e_i = \dfrac{y_{i-1} - y_{i-2}}{x_{i-1} - x_{i-2}} \\
f_i = y_{i-1} - e_i . x_{i-1} \\
m_i = -1/e_i \\
n_i = y_i - m_i . x_i
\end{cases} \tag{8}
$$

$$\Delta_i = (2.d_i.c_i - 2.y_i.c_i - 2.x_i)^2 + 4.\left(x_i^2 + (d_i - y_i)^2 + r^2\right)(c_i + 1) \tag{9}$$

We can take the numbers that vary between i = 1 and 200 points.

N.B: We took into consideration the rest time of the 0.25 s machine. We calculate the Cartesian coordinates X_{si} (x_{si}, y_{si}):

$$
\begin{cases}
x_{si} = \dfrac{-(2.d_i.c_i - 2.c_i.y_i - 2.x_i) \pm \sqrt{\Delta_i}}{2(c_i + 1)} \\
\text{et} \\
y_{si} = c_i.x_i + d_i
\end{cases} \tag{10}
$$

(see **Figures 8 and 9**)

We can calculate the coordinates of the points X_{ai} (x_{ai}, y_{ai}):

$$
\begin{cases}
x_{ai} = \dfrac{x_i + x_{i-1}}{2} \pm a_{oi} . \dfrac{\sqrt{4.r^2 - (x_i - x_{i-1})^2 - (y_i - y_{i-1})^2}}{2\sqrt{a_{oi} + 1}} \\
\text{et} \\
y_{ai} = \dfrac{y_i + y_{i-1}}{2} \pm a_{oi} . \dfrac{\sqrt{4.r^2 - (x_i - x_{i-1})^2 - (y_i - y_{i-1})^2}}{2\sqrt{a_{oi} + 1}}
\end{cases} \tag{11}
$$

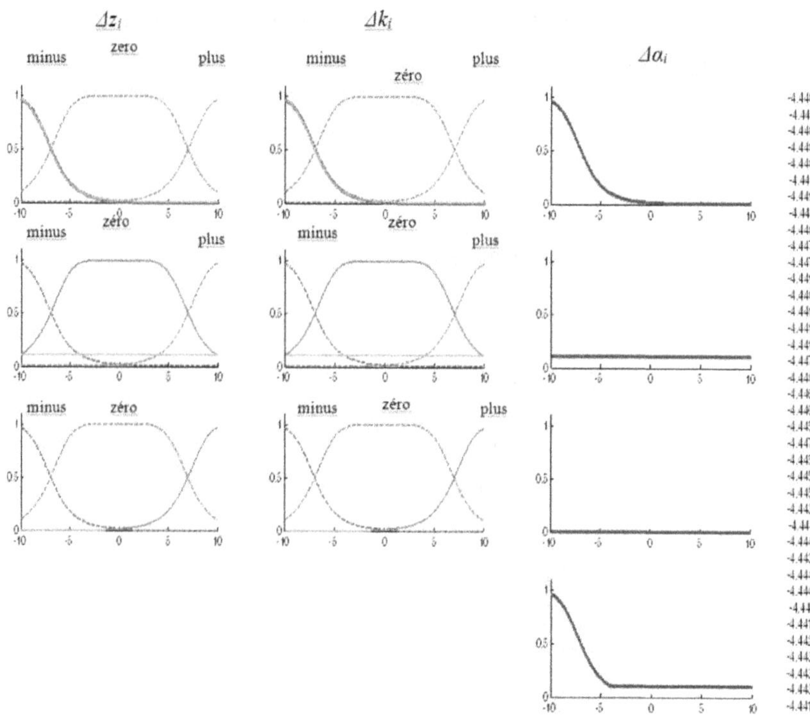

Figure 8. Screen printing of Δz_i, Δk_i, defuzzification, $\Delta \alpha_i$ conclusions according to Mamdani rules [6, 15].

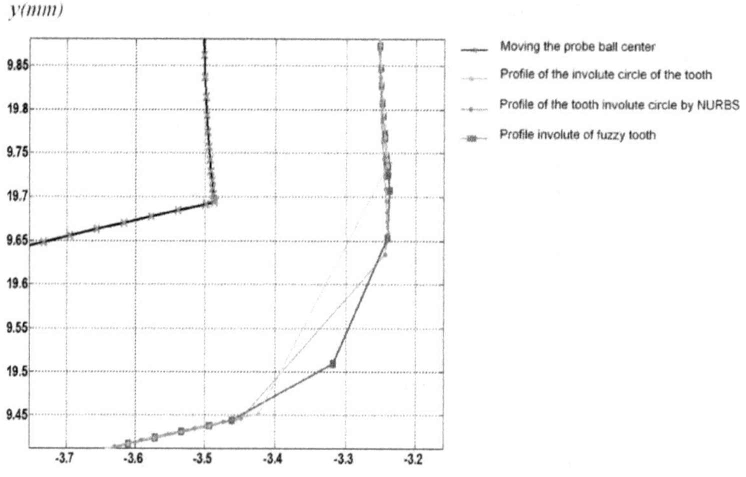

Figure 9. Section A-A.

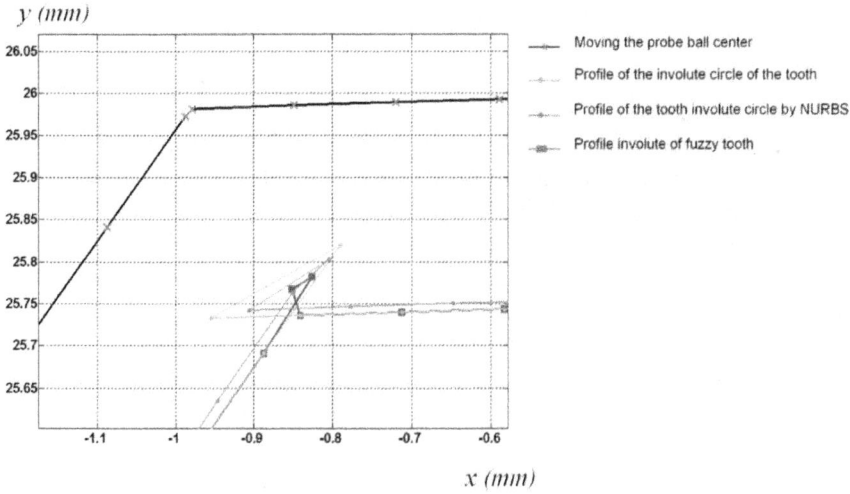

Figure 10. Section B-B.

Then, the values Δz_i, Δk_i are:

$$\begin{cases} \Delta z_i = \sqrt{\left(\left(\frac{d_i - b_i}{a_i - c_i} - x_i\right)^2 + \left(a_i\left(\frac{d_i - b_i}{a_i - c_i} + b_i - y_i\right)\right)^2\right)} \\ \text{et} \\ \Delta k_i = \sqrt{\left(\left(\frac{n_i - f_i}{e_i - m_i} - x_i\right)^2 + \left(e_i\left(\frac{n_i - b_i}{e_i - m_i} + f_i - y_i\right)\right)^2\right)} \end{cases} \qquad (12)$$

(see **Figures 8–10**)

According to the graphs of fuzzy logic, we can conclude the values of $\Delta\alpha_i$ (see **Figure 8**). We calculated Δz_i and Δk_i using the formula of the above relation (13) to calculate these quantities; we determine the values $\Delta\alpha_i$ using fuzzy logic, *max-min* inference, and the generalized function bell and then defuzzification by the centroid method [18] (see **Figure 10**).

In our work, we use the generalized bell shape:

$$y_i = \frac{1}{\left(1 + \left(\left((x_i + 14)/7\right)^3\right)^2\right)} \qquad (13)$$

where z (r) and k (r) represent the values of the linguistic variables of the deviations Δz_i and Δk_i. From these, we deduce the angular difference $\Delta\alpha_i$. **Figure 8** shows an impression of the screen language values define for each input value.

10. Comparison of different sections at the level of the tooth

10.1. Section A-A

After applying the fuzzy logic and plotting the tooth curve, we notice that the green curve is far from the ideal curve; this is the normal vector method. But blue tracing is closer to this one because of having dots that define the involute curve, the red curve is closer to the curve of fuzzy logic (see **Figure 9**).

10.2. Section B-B

In that case, we find that the intersection between the involute curve and the outer circle gives a large deviation as expected. In addition, this leads to an increase in errors, that is, the increase in the gap (see **Figure 10**).

For example, if we determine the height of the tooth by the formula $h = h_a + h_f + \Delta e$ (see **Figure 10**), then the percentage of the error according to the definition can be calculated as follows:

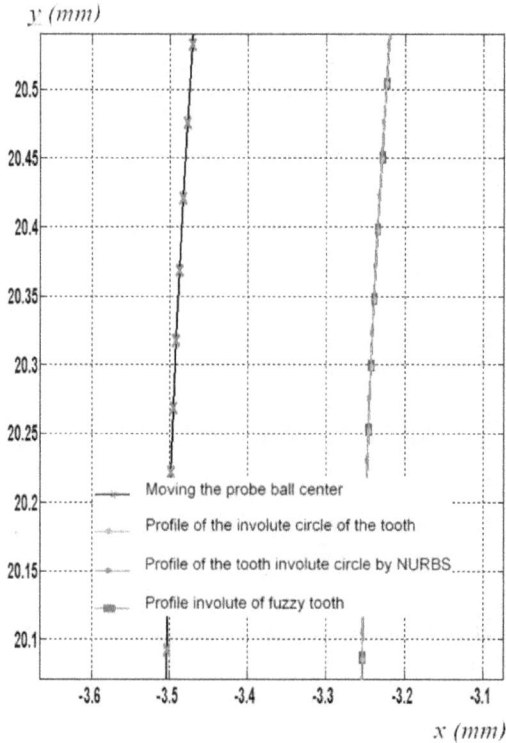

Figure 11. Section C-C.

$$\Delta e_f = f_1 - f_2 = 25,77 - 25,72$$

$$\Delta e_f = 0.05 \text{ mm}$$

$$\Delta e_f\% = 8.33$$

$$\Delta e_g = g_1 - g_2 = 25,82 - 25,72$$

$$\Delta e_g = 0.15 \text{ mm}$$

$$\Delta e_g\% = 25$$

So, it is intolerable to accept miscalculations of more than Δe_g % = 25 by the normal vector method, so the piece was rejected. On the other hand, if we use the same database, we find errors of fuzzy logic for this piece: Δe_f % = 8.33 mm, while the piece was accepted. It was concluded that the fuzzy logic method is closer to the ideal measurement.

10.3. Section C-C

In this case, there is no difference between the two methods (fuzzy logic and the normal vector), the error is zero. However, the method FL does not influence the measurement of spur gears (see **Figures 11** and **12**).

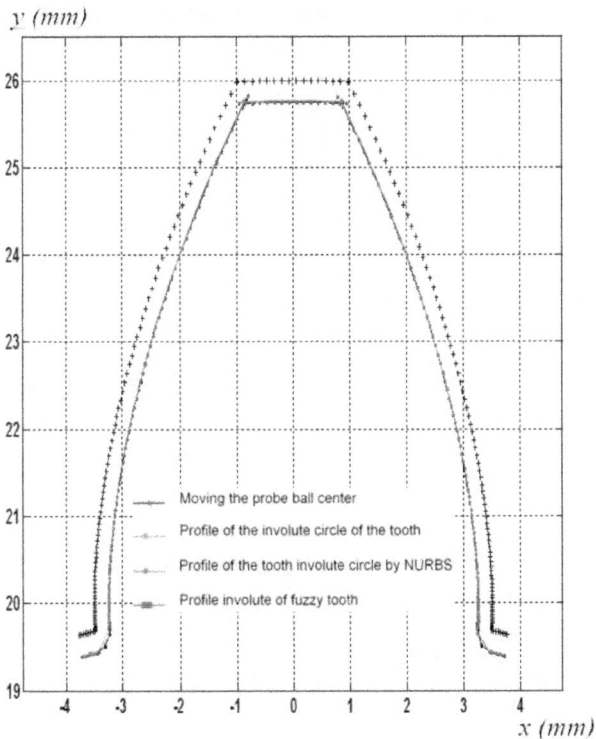

Figure 12. Combination of the x and y coordinates by forming the tooth.

11. Calculation of profile error obtained by the fuzzy logic method

Concluding that the proposed method presents the maximum error in curve peaks, among its values are 0.15, 0.14, 0.1, and 0.1 mm. These peaks have been found to represent intersections between two curves. The weakness of this method is in the intersections of the curves. But in the journey with himself, he does not have any difference.

Indeed, it has been deduced that the result of fuzzy logic is the closest to the ideal curve because of some points that appeared to define the involute curve; at this moment; we could not calculate them by the normal vector method. The graph was constructed by the following formula:

$$\begin{cases} Err_i = \sqrt{\left(x_f - x_v\right)^2 - \left(y_f - y_v\right)^2} \\ Err_i \le \varepsilon_i \end{cases} \tag{14}$$

The fuzzy logic algorithm is used to estimate the actual tooth area of the gears. The performance results given by our approach were compared to the performance of these data using the ideal model.

It is clear that the use of the fuzzy logic estimator is appropriate and estimates the actual area of the tooth which consists of a very complicated path when detecting teeth by CMMs in the sense that the application of the logic technique with estimation of dynamic non-linear systems, special cases, and the surface of the gear which contains several parameters is the best (see **Figure 13**).

Anyway, this problem is solved by this approach. Thus, the role of this work is the determination of the tooth curve to estimate the shape defect of the gears. In our future work, we will try to implement other learning algorithms such as the Kalman estimator or fuzzy neuron.

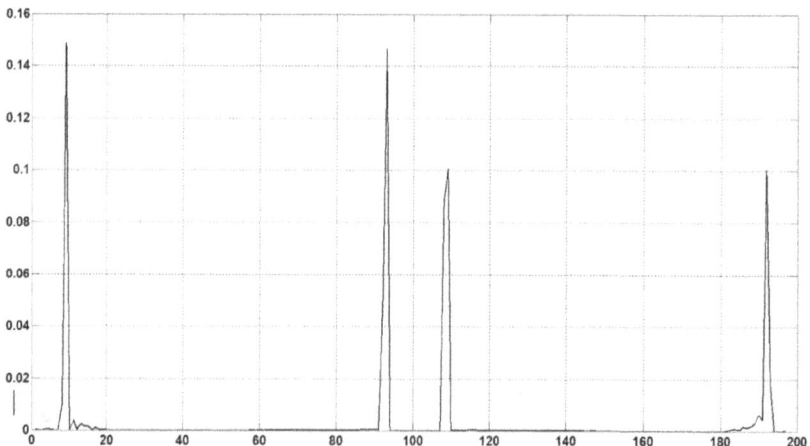

Figure 13. Calculation of the error of the result of the fuzzy logic and the normal vector.

12. Conclusion and perspectives

In this respect, we can conclude that by the principle of fuzzy logic, there is not really the right or the wrong answer as has already been pointed out several times. While the choice of calculation method the profile taken is conditioned between the installation and the performance according to the designer.

Some researchers even suggest averaging the different methods, but this is not a generalization, and the calculations become even more complicated. Finally, we mention that this problem of probing is solved, thanks to the development of the fuzzy logic, which relies on the linguistic knowledge, nonlinearity, and not the needs of the model; the solution was obtained by means of a computer. Nevertheless, it lacks precise guidelines for the design, because of contradictory inference rules.

Author details

Bloul Benattia

Address all correspondence to: bloul.benattia@univ-boumerdes.dz

Reliability Laboratory of Petroleum Equipment and Materials-Boumerdes, M'hamed Bougara University of Boumerdès, Boumerdes, Algeria

References

[1] Wozniak A, Mayer JRR, Balazinski M. Stylus tip envelop method: corrected measured point determination in high definition coordinate metrology. International Journal of Advanced Manufacturing Technology. 2009;**42**:505-514

[2] Bloul B, Bourdim A. Control inspection involute curve of gear tooth of pinion type cutter using the fuzzy logic. International Journal of Metrology and Quality Engineering. 2012;**3**: 47-54

[3] Achiche S, Fan Z, Baron L, Wozniak A, Balazinski M, Sorensen T. 3D CMM strain-gauge triggering probe error characteristics modeling using fuzzy logic. IEEE; 2008

[4] Wozniak A, Dobosz. Methods of testing of static in-accuracy of the CMM scanning probe. Metrology and Measurement Systems. 2003;**10**(2):191-203

[5] Ginnity SM, Irwin GW. Fuzzy logic approach to manoeuvring target tracking. IEE Proceedings - Radar, Sonar and Navigation. 1998;**145**(6):337-341

[6] Wozniak A, Mayer R, Balazinski M. Application of Fuzzy Knowledge Base for Corrected Measured Point Determination in Coordinate Metrology. IEEE; 2007

[7] Li ZX, Gou JB, Chu XY. Geometric algorithms for work piece localization. IEEE Transactions on Robotics and Automation. 1996;**14**:864-878

[8] Bloul B, Bourdim A, Karoui A, Bourdim M. Determination deformities gears involute of coordinate measuring machines. In: International Seminar on Mechanical Technologies; Tlemcen, Algeria; 2009

[9] Irwin GW, Mc Ginnity S. Fuzzy logic approach to manoeuvring target tracking. IEE Proceedings - Radar, Sonar and Navigation. 1998;**145**(6):337-341

[10] Jang J-SR, Sun C-T, Mizutani E. Neuro-Fuzzy and Soft Computing a Computational Approach to Learning and Machine Integence. Library of Congress Cataloging in Publication Data; 1997

[11] Weimin P, Yi L, Jishun L. Control of analogue scan probe in CMM inspect of spiral bevel gear. IEEE; 2006

[12] Hung C-C, Ferndndee RB. Minimizing rules of fuzzy logic system by using a systematic approach. IEEE; 1993

[13] Balazinski M, Bellerose M. Czogala Application of fuzzy logic techniques to the selection of cutting parameters in machining processes. In: Fuzzy Sets System. IEEE; 1994

[14] Brazhkin BS, Mirotvorskii VS. Calculation of curved surfaces on coordinate measuring machine. Measurement Techniques. 2005;**7**:21-24

[15] Wozniak A. Application of piezotranslator for the dy-namic testing of scanning probes in coordinate measuring machines. Mecatronica. 2004

[16] Chen C-W. Modeling and control for nonlinear struc-tural systems via NN-based approach. Expert Systems with Applications. 2009

[17] Chen C-Y, Lin J-W, Lee W-I, Chen C-W. Fuzzy control for an oceanic structure: A case study intime-delay TLP system. Journal of Vibration and Control. 2010:147-160

[18] Bloul B, Bourdim A, Aour B, Harhout R. Measurement default diagnostics of a roughness meter with TS100 head using a rectified specimen and solved by fuzzy logic estimator. International Journal of Advanced Manufacturing Technology. 2017;**92**(1-4):673-684

Chapter 5

Fuzzy Controller-Based MPPT of PV Power System

M. Venkateshkumar

Additional information is available at the end of the chapter

http://dx.doi.org/10.5772/intechopen.80065

Abstract

The power demand has been increasing day by day due to population growth, new industrial development, etc. Meeting power demand is one of the challenge factors for fossil fuel-based power generation alone as well as the environmental issue of carbon footprint. Consequently, there is a need to concentrate on alternate energy sources to meet the power demand. In this chapter, the photovoltaic (PV) cell operation under various weather conditions is analysed, and based on the performance, the MPPT controller is developed by using fuzzy logic controller. The proposed system has been modelled in MATLAB environment, and the system performance has been analysed. Finally, the simulation results are evaluated and compared with IEEE 1547 standard for proving the effectiveness of the proposed system.

Keywords: MPPT, fuzzy, PV, MATLAB

1. Introduction

The maximum power point tracking (MPPT) plays a major role in photovoltaic (PV) power system. The PV power generation changes with respect to sun light irradiance and temperature [1]. Nowadays, many researches develop different MPPT techniques for improving the MPP in PV system. There are two major classifications such as indirect and direct MPPT controllers [2]. The indirect MPPT techniques are used for offline analysis of PV system performance, while the direct MPPT techniques are used to measure PV voltage and PV current during online condition. In this chapter, the direct method has been developed by using fuzzy logic controller to track the MPP of PV system [3]. This method is very robust and easy; meanwhile, no mathematical model is required for designing the controller. In this chapter, MPPT algorithm has been tested with numerical simulation in MATLAB environment, and the PV performance at constant and variable irradiance as well as temperature has been analysed [4].

2. Mathematical modelling of PV system

The following mathematical models of electrical characteristics are considered to design 20 kW photovoltaic module and simulated using MATLAB environment:

2.1. Open-circuit voltage

The open-circuit voltage, V_{OC}, is the extreme voltage offered from a PV cell, and this happens at zero current. The open-circuit voltage links to the amount of forward bias on the PV cell due to the bias of the PV cell junction with the light-generated current [5, 6]:

$$V = \frac{NKT}{Q} \, in \, \frac{I_L - I_o}{I_o} + 1 \text{ Volt} \tag{1}$$

where V is the open-circuit voltage, N is diode ideality constant, K is the Boltzmann constant $(1.381*10^{\wedge}\text{-}23 \text{ J/K})$, T is temperature in Kelvin, Q is electron charge $(1.602*10^{\wedge}\text{-}19 \text{ c})$, IL is the light-generated current same as Iph (A), and Io is the saturation diode current (A).

2.2. Light-generated current (radiation)

$$I_L = \frac{G}{G_{ref}} * \left(I_{Lref} + \alpha_{Isc}(T_c - T_{c\,ref}) \right) \tag{2}$$

where G is the radiation (W/m²), Gref is the radiation under standard condition 1000 W/m², ILref is the photoelectric current under standard condition 0.15 A, TCref is module temperature under standard condition 298 K, αISC is the temperature coefficient of the short-circuit current (A/K) = 0.0065/K, and IL is the light-generated current (radiation).

2.3. Reverse saturation current

$$I_o = I_{or} * (T/T_{ref})^3 \exp\left(\left(\tfrac{QE_g}{KN} \right) * \left(\tfrac{1}{T} , \tfrac{1}{T} \right) \right) \tag{3}$$

$$I_{orn} = \frac{Isc}{\exp^{(V_{oc}/NV_s)}} \tag{4}$$

where Io is the reverse saturated current, Ior is the saturation current, N is the ideality factor 1.5, and Eg is the band gap for silicon 1.10 eV.

2.4. Short-circuit current

Ish = IL. It is the extreme value of the current produced by a PV cell. It is formed by the short circuit-situation: V = 0.

$$I_{sh} = I_L - I_o\left(\left(\exp^{\left(Q\frac{V - IR_s}{NKT} \right)} - 1 \right) \right) \tag{5}$$

2.5. Irradiation

G = radiation W/m^2 (**Figures 1** and **2**).

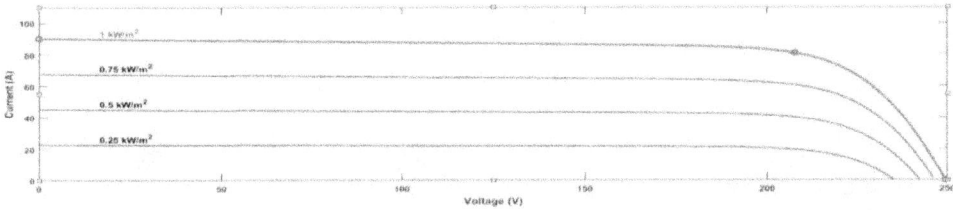

Figure 1. PV—Voltage vs. current characteristics.

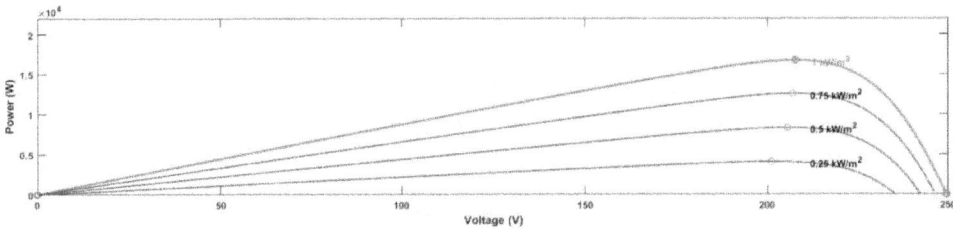

Figure 2. PV—Power vs. voltage characteristics.

3. Maximum power point tracking (MPPT) for photovoltaic system

Renewable energy sources play an important role in meeting consumer power demand due to their abundant availability and lesser impact on the environment [5]. The main hurdle in PV energy expansion is the investment cost of the PV power system implementation. PV energy generation is not constant throughout the day due to the changes in weather. The efficiency of power generation is very low (the range of efficiency is only 9–17% in low irradiation regions). Therefore, MPPT technologies have an important role in PV power generation for optimal power generation at various weather conditions.

In this chapter, we have discussed and analysed fuzzy logic controller-based MPPT controller for 20 kW PV system.

The proposed fuzzy-based MPPT block diagram is shown in **Figure 3**. **Figure 4** presents the structure of the fuzzy controller that has two inputs and one output. The fuzzy membership function has been designed by trapezoidal method for both input and output membership values. The defuzzification of proposed fuzzy controller has been used for centre of gravity. The MPPT fuzzy controller has two inputs such as PV voltage and PV current shown in **Figures 5** and **6**, respectively. The MPPT fuzzy controller generates a duty cycle based on input of fuzzy controller and is fed into boost converter shown in **Figure 7**. Finally, the fuzzy interference rules are designed based on changes in PV voltage

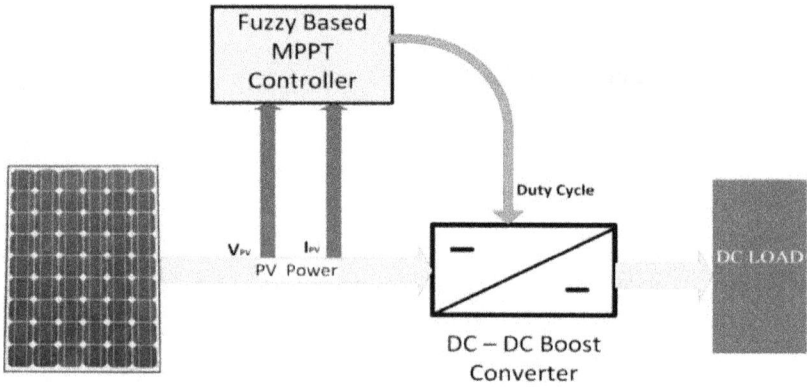

Figure 3. PV—MPPT block diagram.

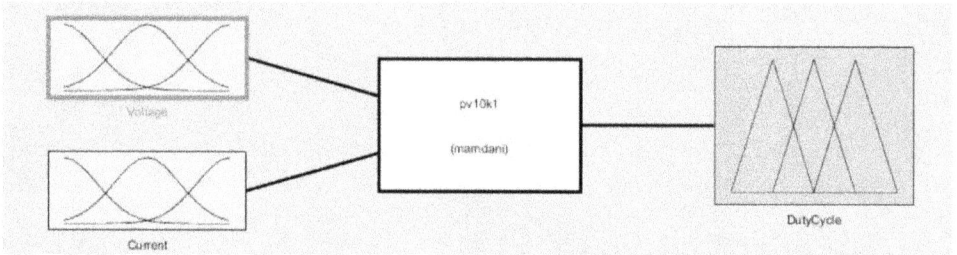

Figure 4. Fuzzy controller structure for MPPT of PV system.

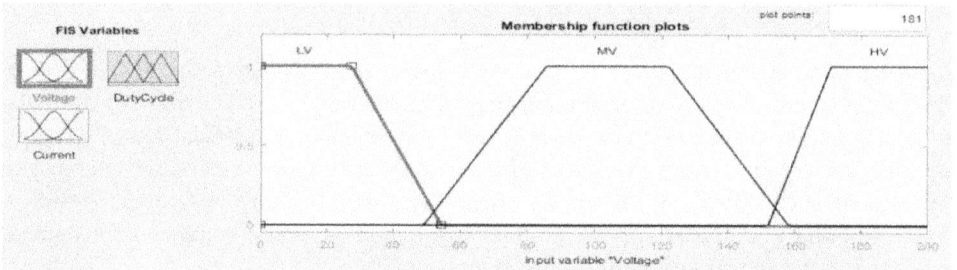

Figure 5. Fuzzy input membership function (voltage) for MPPT of PV system.

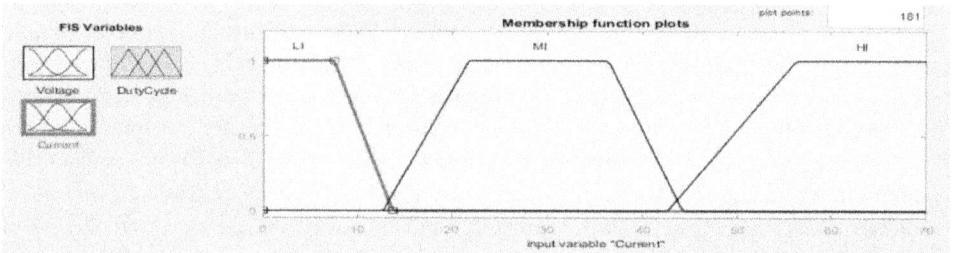

Figure 6. Fuzzy input membership function (current) for MPPT of PV system.

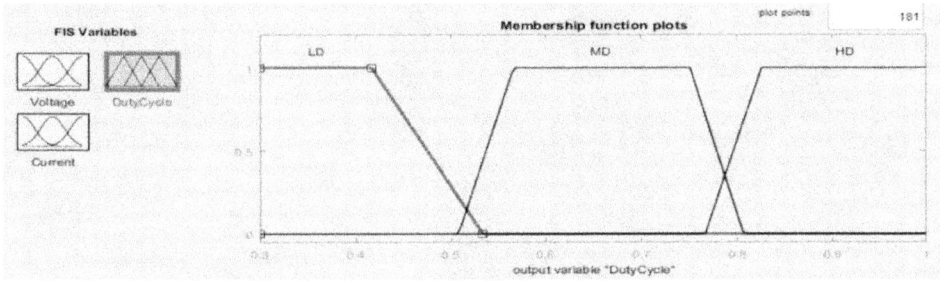

Figure 7. Fuzzy output membership function (duty cycle) for MPPT of PV system.

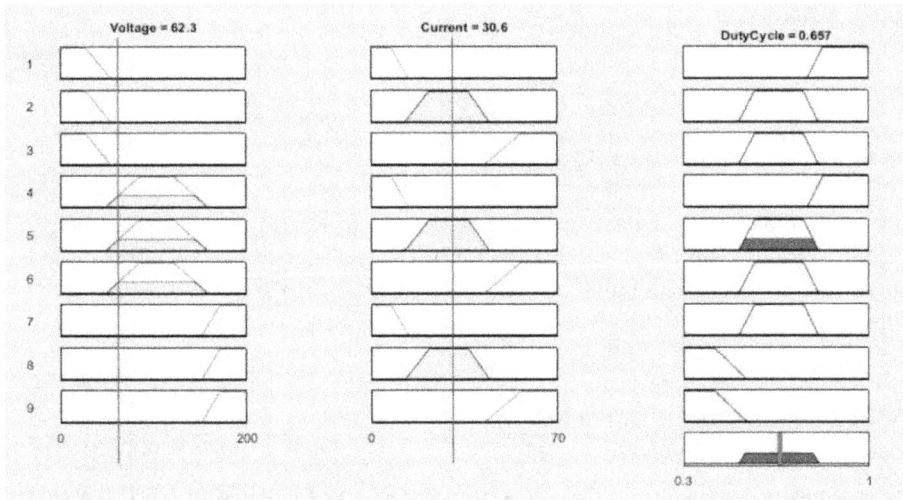

Figure 8. Fuzzy rules for MPPT of PV system.

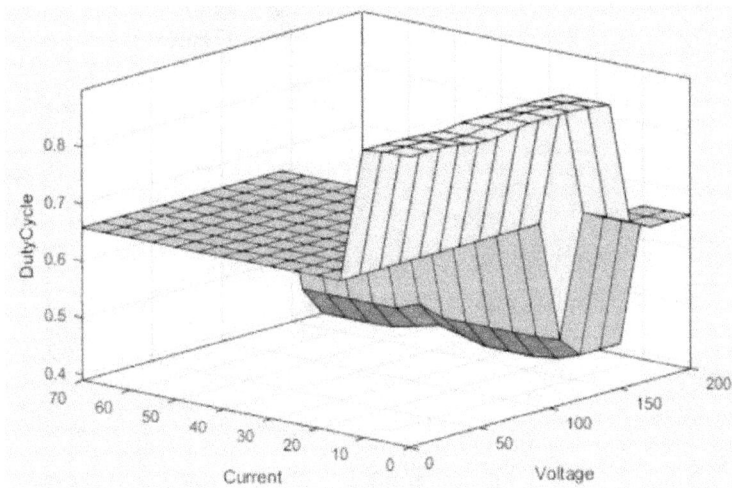

Figure 9. Fuzzy surface structure for MPPT of PV system.

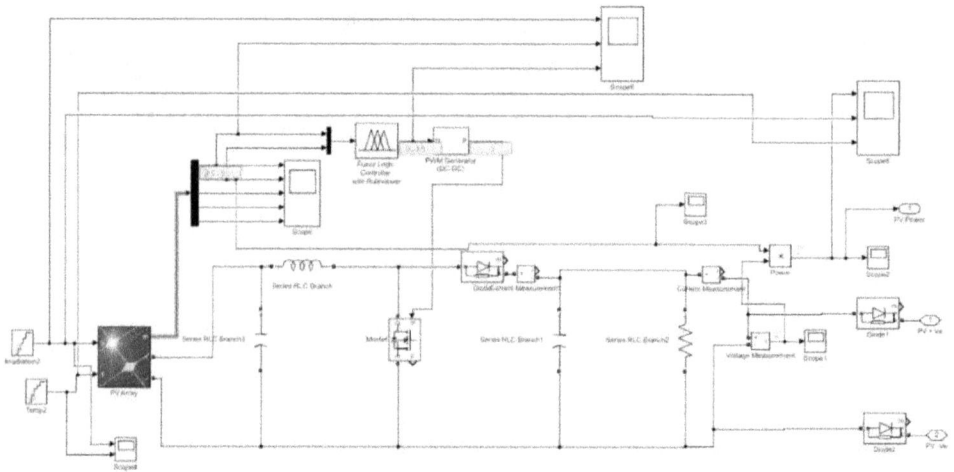

Figure 10. Fuzzy simulation model for MPPT of PV system.

and current under various weather conditions as shown in **Figure 8**, and then the surface view of fuzzy rules is presented in **Figure 9**. The above designed fuzzy controller has been implemented in MATLAB simulation of 20 kW PV system and its boost converter as shown in **Figure 10**.

4. MPPT results and discussion

The developed fuzzy logic controller has been tested and simulated in MATLAB environment, and the fuzzy controller performance under various weather conditions such as variable irradiance (1000, 750, 500 and 250 W/m²) and temperature (20, 25, 30, 32 and 35°C) was analysed. The simulated results are analysed in the above conditions. **Figure 11** represented PV boost converter output voltage at various irradiance. **Figure 12** represented PV boost

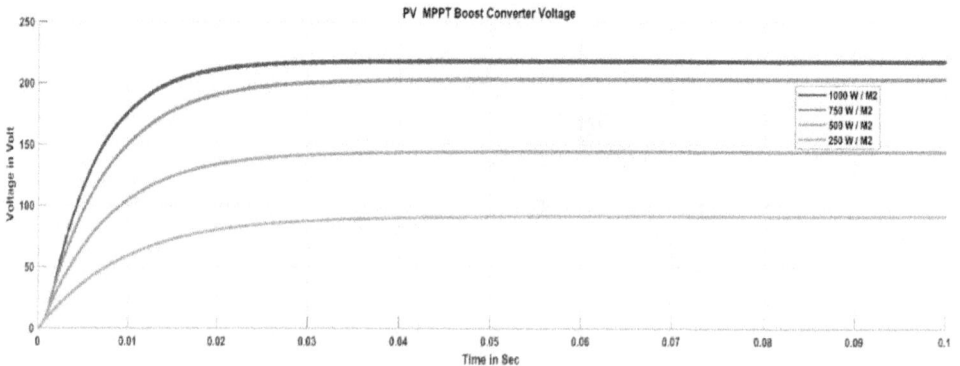

Figure 11. Fuzzy-based 20 kW PV system output voltage at various irradiance.

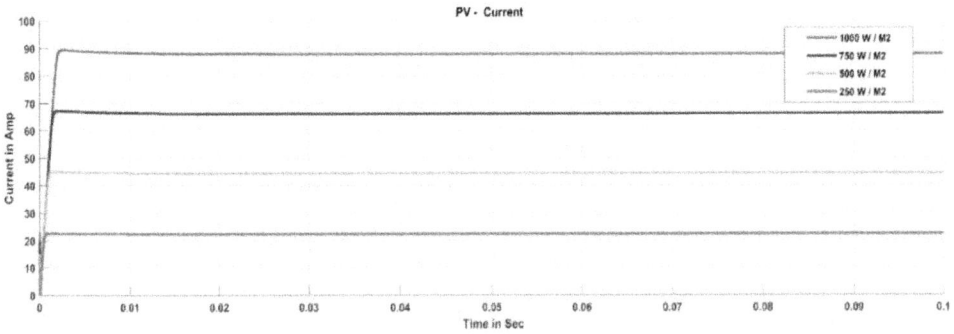

Figure 12. Fuzzy-based 20 kW PV system output current at various irradiance.

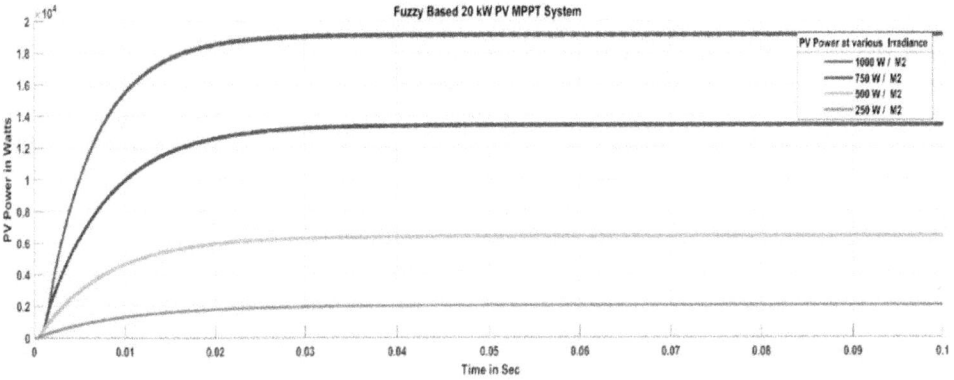

Figure 13. Fuzzy-based 20 kW PV system output power at various irradiance.

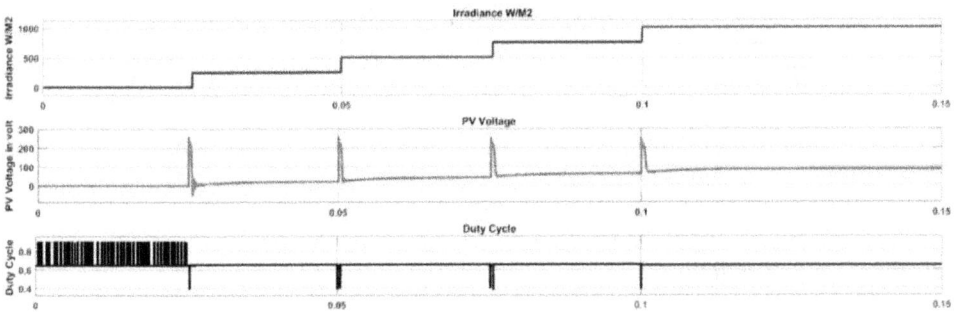

Figure 14. Duty cycle generation at various weather conditions.

converter output current at various irradiance. **Figure 13** represented PV boost converter output power at various irradiance. The fuzzy controller output signal of boost converter duty cycle is analysed at various weather conditions shown in **Figure 14**. The proposed MPPT system has been analysed in two different cases such as Case 1 (constant temperature and

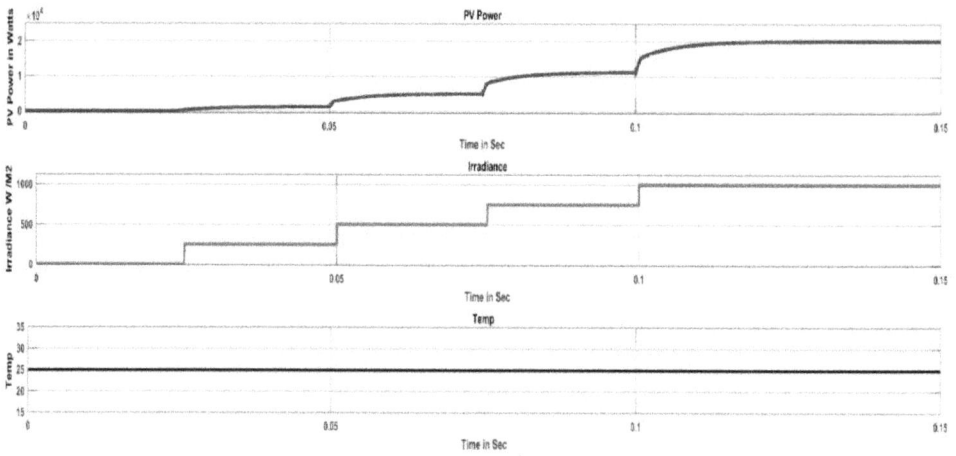

Figure 15. Analysis of the PV system performance at constant temperature.

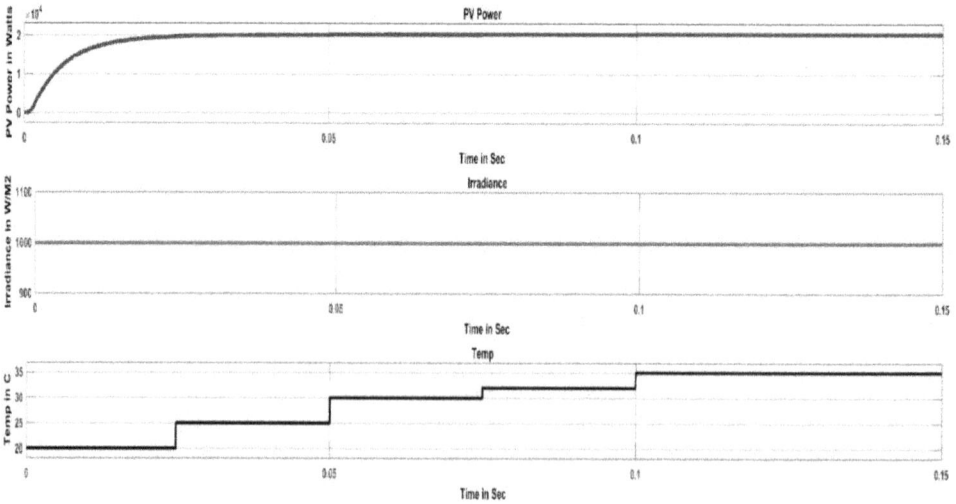

Figure 16. Analysis of the PV system performance at constant irradiance.

variable irradiance shown in **Figure 15**) and Case 2 (constant irradiance and variable temperature shown in **Figure 16**).

5. Conclusion

This paper deals with grid integration of PV power system with intelligent controller-
based energy management to improve the power quality. The above objectives are
achieved by modelling of mathematical design of PV system and simulating PV system

at various weather conditions with fuzzy-based MPPT system. The fuzzy-based energy management system is developed and tested under various power demands, and then operation of battery charging and discharging is analysed. Finally, the proposed objective of grid integration of PV system is simulated in MATLAB, and system performance under various operating conditions is analysed. The improvement of power quality simulation results is compared with 1547 standard and proves the effectiveness of the proposed system.

Author details

M. Venkateshkumar[1,2*]

*Address all correspondence to: venkatmme@ieee.org

1 IEEE Young Professional, Madras Section, India

2 Department of EEE, AVIT, Chennai, Tamil Nadu, India

References

[1] Kumar A, Chaudhary P, Rizwan M. Development of fuzzy logic based MPPT controller for PV system at varying meteorological parameters. In: 2015 Annual IEEE India Conference (INDICON); New Delhi; 2015. pp. 1-6

[2] Mishra S, Sekhar PC. TS fuzzy based adaptive perturb algorithm for MPPT of a grid connected single stage three phase VSC interfaced PV generating system. In: 2012 IEEE Power and Energy Society General Meeting; San Diego, CA; 2012. pp. 1-7

[3] Al Nabulsi A, Dhaouadi R. Efficiency optimization of a DSP-based standalone PV system using fuzzy logic and dual-MPPT control. IEEE Transactions on Industrial Informatics. 2012;8(3):573-584

[4] Xie W, Hui J. MPPT for PV system based on a novel fuzzy control strategy. In: 2010 International Conference on Digital Manufacturing & Automation; ChangSha; 2010. pp. 960-963

[5] Anandhakumar G, Venkateshkumar M, Shankar P. Intelligent controller based MPPT method for the photovoltaic power system. In: 2013 International Conference on Human Computer Interactions (ICHCI); Chennai; 2013. pp. 1-6

[6] Indumathi R, Venkateshkumar M, Raghavan R. Integration of D-Statcom based photovoltaic cell power in low voltage power distribution grid. In: IEEE-International Conference on Advances in Engineering, Science and Management (ICAESM-2012); Nagapattinam, Tamil Nadu; 2012. pp. 460-465

An Integrated Multicriteria and Fuzzy Logic Approach for Municipal Solid Waste Landfill Siting

Abdelwaheb Aydi

Additional information is available at the end of the chapter

http://dx.doi.org/10.5772/intechopen.75161

Abstract

Landfill site selection should take into account a wide range of alternative and evalua-tion criteria in order to reduce negative impacts on the environment. This study presents a geographic information systems-based multicriteria site selection of municipal solid waste (MSW) landfill in Ariana Region, Tunisia. The multicriteria decision integrates constraints and factors to select MSW landfill suitability. The methodology is used for ranking the best suitable landfill sites by the integration of fuzzy logic and analytic hier-archy process (AHP). The fuzzy set theory is used to standardize criteria using different fuzzy membership functions while the AHP is used to establish the relative importance of the criteria. The AHP makes pairwise comparisons of relative importance between hierarchy elements assembled by environmental and socio-economic decision criteria. The landfill suitability is accomplished by applying weighted linear combination (WLC) that uses a comparison matrix to aggregate different importance scenarios associated with environmental and socio-economic objectives. Data were assorted into five suitabil-ity classes within the study area, i.e., high, suitable, moderate, low and very low suitabil-ity areas, which represented 5.4, 0.5, 12.5, 3.9 and 2.5%, of the study area, respectively. Additionally, 75.2% was considered to be completely unsuitable for a landfill site. As a result, two candidate landfill sites are suggested.

Keywords: MSW landfill, GIS, multicriteria, analytical hierarchy process

1. Introduction

The construction of sanitary landfills that comply with environmental legislation and that reduce the undesired effects of current practices is one of the main municipal solid wastes (MSW) management priorities in Tunisia. The first and most important step in planning solid waste landfill is the site selection for solid waste disposal [1]. Landfill site selection is a complicated, complex, monotonous, requiring evaluation of various criteria. Among those criteria economic, environmental and social property are often considered for attractive the scheduling process and for setting guidelines that reduce public health risks, impact to the environment, cost to facility users and inefficiencies connected with other services [2–4]. As such, it evidently requires the processing of a massive amount of spatial data [5]. Various landfill siting techniques have been developed for this purpose. In the last few years, geographic information systems (GIS) have been increasingly used to facilitate and lower the cost of the process of selecting sites for sanitary landfills [6]. A number of GIS methods and techniques have been proposed to evaluate suitable landfill locations [1, 2, 7–9]. Some of those techniques take advantage of GIS-based multicriteria evaluation (MCE) [1, 2, 7, 8, 5, 10] and fuzzy set theory [2, 4, 11]. In MCE, the weighted linear combination (WLC) is one of the most popular methods because of its simplicity [12]. Several WLC-based approaches for landfill siting can be found in the literature [5, 11, 13]. In the WLC procedure, analytical hierarchy process (AHP) [14] is often applied to elicit criteria weights and to enhanced represent interaction between criteria and alternatives [6]. In AHP, weights are computed based on pairwise judgments and checked for consistency. Because pairwise judgments are often biased and inconsistent, acceptable consistency ratio (CR) often requires iterative revisions of the pairwise judgments before the final weights are computed.

The purpose of this paper is to evaluate the suitability of the study region to optimally site a landfill for MSW Ariana using AHP and WLC in a GIS environment.

2. Materials and methods

2.1. Study area

The study area is the Ariana Region, located in the north-eastern part of the Republic of Tunisia (**Figure 1**). The region occupies 482 km² and borders Bizerte government to the north, Tunisia government to the south, Manouba government to the West and Mediterranean Sea to the East. This is the fastest growing region in the country that has experienced a significant population growth especially in the past few decades. This densely populated region (876 people per km2) includes 90.8% of its area being urban and the remaining 9.2% being rural with a total population that exceeds 510,500 people or 4.8% of the total country's population [15].

The climate is Mediterranean, characterized by dry and warm summers, and cool, wet winters. The average annual precipitation is 450 mm/year and much of the precipitation falls in late autumn and early winter where the month of November has the highest precipitation while August has the lowest. The annual predominant wind direction in Ariana region is northward with an annual average wind speed of 1.5 m/s.

Currently, the MSW disposal in the region is based on landfilling in the sanitary landfill of Jebel Chakir, located 15 km to the south of Ariana city. The Jebel Chakir landfill will be closed in the near future and is too far from waste production centers in Ariana region, which increase

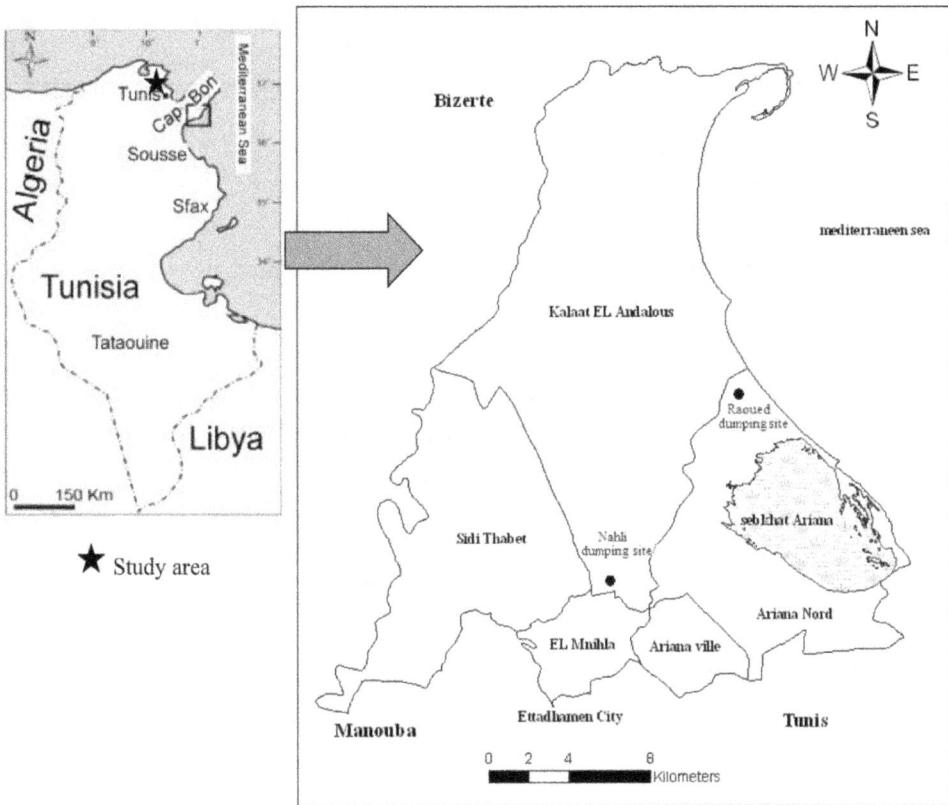

Figure 1. Location of the study area.

the transportation cost and need additional investments in the infrastructure of roads, hence intensify the financial problems of the responsible authorities. The estimated solid waste for the Ariana Region is 4,251,783 tons for exploitation period of 20 years. The estimate is quantified on the basis of average rate of daily waste production of 0.6 kg per capita [16]. The estimate assumes an efficiency of collecting waste of 95, and 1% of annual increase of waste production per capita per year. The estimated capacity needed for landfill area is 28 ha using average compacted waste density of 950 kg/m^3 and cover material [17].

2.2. Methodology

Hierarchical organization of the constraints and criteria considered for the landfill suitability is shown in **Table 1**. The top of the hierarchy is the goal while subsequent levels describe the decision or analysis criteria, the constraints and factors in increasing detail. The goal is to identify the areas that are most suitable for landfill siting.

In this work, the environmental, social, economic and geological information are considered to be pertinent in defining the potential sites to create a MSW landfill. In the ArcView GIS,

Level 1 Goal	Level 2 Decision factors	Level 3 Subfactors	Exclusion criteria	Appreciation criteria
Landfill suitability	Geology	Soil permeability	*	
		Elevation	*	
		Slope	*	
		Distance from coastal zone	*	
	Hydro/Hydrogeology	Depth to ground water table	*	
		Distance from water supply (reservoirs, wells, boreholes, springs)	*	
		Distance from wetlands	*	
		Distance from rivers	*	
		Distance from irrigation canals	*	
	Environment	Land use	*	*
		Olfactory and sonorous impacts		*
		Distance from protected areas	*	
	Social	Proximity to dense population		*
		Distance from residential areas	*	
	Economic	Proximity to roads	*	*
		Proximity to building materials	*	

Table 1. Hierarchical structure for the selection of the MSW landfill site.

all the thematic maps were transformed on raster grid to be used by Idrisi software. A raster grid cell of 100×100 m^2 was generated. Each cell is considered as a homogenous unit for any given factor. All the factors influenced were standardized and weighed and then combined using the AHP methods.

The site selection process is implemented in the following steps:

- The Exclusion of restricted areas for landfill siting. The constraints based on the Boolean criteria were used to differentiate areas that can be considered suitable for a waste disposal site from those that cannot be considered suitable under any conditions

- The factors were standardized to a continuous scale of suitability from 0 (least suitable) to 10 (most suitable) in a GIS environment by fuzzy membership functions, then weighted and combined using the AHP methods.

- The WLC aggregation method was applied for preparing the suitability maps. Suitability maps for each set of factors were combined to create three scenarios to allow determination of the most suitable sites.

- The landfill suitability is classified in five equally scored classes: high, suitable, moderate, low and very low suitability areas

3. Classification of exclusion criteria (constraints).

The exclusion criteria are constraints having for objective to limit research of suitable sites which do not tolerate any competition [10].

The classification consists in selecting various areas that represents a new plan of information for a required condition. Maps were classified into two categories: 1 was ranked to zones verifying the condition and 0 was ranked to the other zones. The resulting image is a Boolean image.

The last step consisted in combining, by superposition, the information contained in Boolean layers relative to the exclusion criteria mentioned above. The logical operator "AND" has been used in this part; it translates the intersection between conditions that must be absolutely satisfied.

4. Standardization of appreciation criteria

MCE requires that the values contained in the different criterion map layers be transformed to similar units [11]. A number of approaches can be used to make criterion map layers comparable. The fuzzy membership approach is one of the standardization methods that have been proposed [10]. For this reason, fuzzy sets were used in this study. To apply fuzzy functions in the GIS environment in this case study, all the map layers are transformed to a raster format with 100 m pixel size. Four fuzzy set membership functions are provided in IDRISI: Sigmoidal, J-Shaped, Linear and User-defined. Our choice has been made relying on two types of factors (environmental and socio-economic) that have been standardized in one common interval from ranging from 0 to 10.

5. Weighting factors for aggregation

The purpose of criterion weighting is to express the importance of each criterion relative to other criteria. One of the techniques that can be used in assigning weights is Pairwise Comparisons (that characterizes analytic hierarchy process: AHP, developed by Saaty [18]; it determines accurate relative weights of indicators by allowing to divide the complex decision problem into a series of one-on-one judgments regarding the significance of each criterion relative to the others.

Intensity of importance	Definition
1	Equal importance
3	Weak importance of one over another
5	Essential or strong importance
7	Demonstrated importance
9	Absolute importance
2,4,6,8	Intermediate values between adjacent judgments the two
Reciprocals of above non zero	If activity (i) has one of the above nonzero numbers assigned to it when compared with activity (j), then (j)has the reciprocal value when compared with (i)

Table 2. The comparison scale in AHP Saaty [14].

The pairwise comparison involves three tasks: (1) developing a comparison matrix at each level of the hierarchy initial from the second level and functioning down, (2) computing the relative weights for each element of the hierarchy and (3) estimating the consistency ratio to check the consistency of the judgment [19]. In the AHP weight can be derived by taking the principal eigenvector of a square reciprocal matrix of pair-wise comparisons between the criteria. The method uses a scale with values range from 1 to 9, illustrated in **Table 2**.

The consistency ratio is one of the very important aspects of the AHP theory. It allows us to assess the overall consistency of all pairwise comparison judgments provided by the decision makers in the form of pairwise comparison judgment matrices. More formally, the consistency ratio (CR) is calculated through dividing the consistency index (CI) by the randomized index (RI).

The consistency index (CI) for each matrix can be expressed as:$CI = (\lambda_{max} - n)/(n - 1)$; Where λ_{max} is the principal eigenvalue of the judgment matrix and n is its order Saaty [18].

Then, the consistency ratio (CR) is defined as follows: $CR = CI/RI$; Where RI is the random index and depends on the number of elements being compared Saaty [18]. If CR < 0.10, the ratio indicates a reasonable level of consistency in the pairwise comparison; however, if $CR \geq 0.10$, it indicates inconsistent judgments [18]. Once the satisfactory CR is obtained, the resultant weights are applied.

6. MCE using WLC method

A multicriteria evaluation consists of combining a set of criteria (constraints and factors) to build a single suitability map according to a specific category (set of factors). One of the most common procedures for aggregating data is the weighted linear combination (WLC) [19].

WLC is a technique based on the concept of a weighted average in which continuous criteria are standardized to a common numeric range, and then combined by means of a weighted average to produce a continuous mapping of suitability [13].

The suitability index for a site is the sum of the products of the standardized score for each criterion multiplied by the weight of each criterion, the following equation is given by Eastman [20]:

$$S = \sum_{i=1}^{n} w_i x_i$$

where S is the suitability index for area i; w_1, w_2...,w_n are the weights of the criteria constrained to sum to 1; x_1, x_2...,x_n are the standardized scores of the criteria i and n is the total number of criteria. As the sum of the weights is constrained to one, the final combined estimate is presented on the same scale.

7. Results and discussions

7.1. Criteria description and application

In Tunisia, there is not a Solid Waste Control Regulations for disposal site. Hence, criteria were selected according the MSW landfill siting guidelines of the countries legislation, extensive literature review, [1–4, 7, 9, 11, 13] assessment via questionnaire; availability of the data and local expert.

7.1.1. Exclusive criteria (constraints)

In this study, 13 constraints criteria such as: (1) Soil permeability, (2) Elevation, (3) Slope, (4) Distance from coastal zone,(5) Depth to ground water table, (6) Distance from water supply (reservoirs, wells, boreholes, springs), (7) Distance from wetlands, (8) Distance from rivers, (9) Distance from irrigation canals, (10) Land use, (11) Proximity to roads, (12) Distance from protected areas, and (13) Distance from residential areas were selected for the computation process. The buffer zones in the different constraint layers are listed in **Table 3**.

Figure 2 shows the maps layers of all the constraints criteria after buffering and restriction.

7.1.2. Appreciation criteria (factors)

The next process is to further examine the suitable areas for landfill. Factor criteria were used in order to further evaluate those areas.

7.1.3. Environmental factor

7.1.3.1. Land use

Land use is important for resolving public conflicts over the acceptance of unwanted facility siting [4]. **Table 4** shows the membership values assigned to all categories used in the analysis based on results of investigations with experts (agronomist, environmentalists…).

Constraints	Buffering
Soil permeability	Exclude soils having high rate of permeability
Elevation	Exclude areas over 200 m
Slope	Exclude areas over 5%
Distance from coastal zone	3 km buffer zone
Depth to ground water table	Exclude depth less than 14 m
Distance from water supply (reservoirs, wells, boreholes, springs)	3 km buffer zone
Distance from wetlands	1 km buffer zone
Distance from rivers	200 m buffer zone
Distance from irrigation canals	200 m buffer zone
Land use	Exclude arable lands and area with high economic advantages
Distance from protected areas	300 m buffer zone
Distance from residential areas	2 km buffer zone
Proximity to roads	200 m buffer zone

Table 3. Buffer zones for the generation of constraint map.

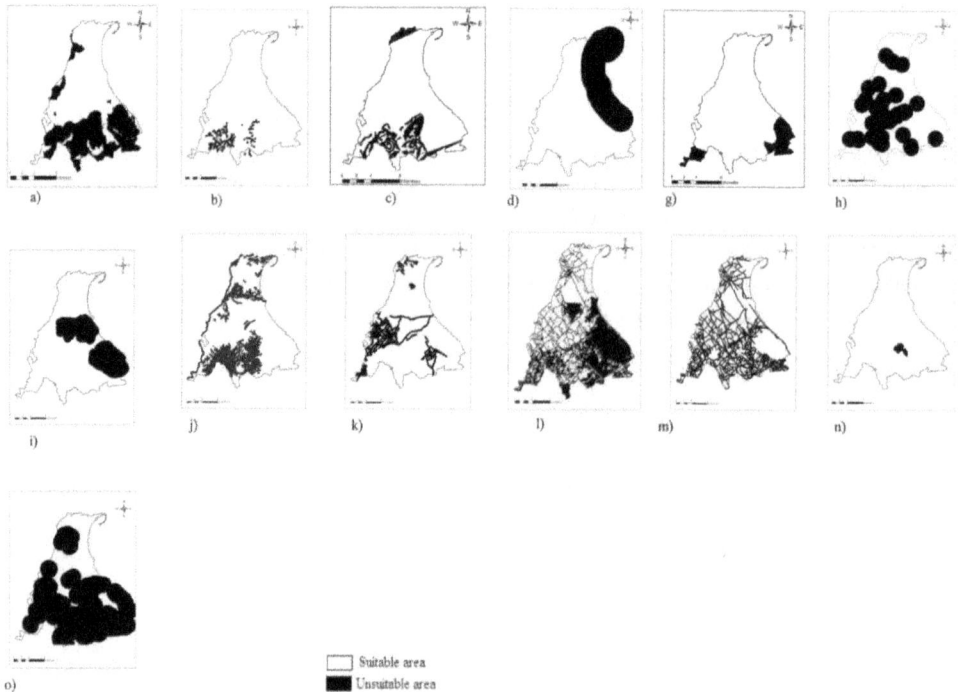

Figure 2. Boolean images of constraints maps a) Soil permeability, b) Elevation, c) Slope, d) Distance from coastal Zone, g) Depth to ground water Table, h) Distance from water supply, i) Distance from wetlands, j) Distance from rivers, k) Distance from irrigation canals, l) Land use, m) Distance from roads, n) Distance from protected areas, o) Distance from residential areas.

Factors	Sub-factors	Standardization of factors	
		Control point	Fuzzy function/membership
Environmental	Land use (no units)		
	Urban areas		0
	Protected area		0
	Wetlands		0
	Water		0
	Vine		2
	Mariachi culture		2
	Cereals		3
	Olive trees		3
	Forager culture		4
	Course		6
	Naked soil		10
	Olfactory and sonorous impacts	200 and 3000 m	Linear, increasing
Socio-economic	Proximity to dense population	200 and 1000 inhabitants/km²	Sigmoidal, decreasing
	Proximity to buildings materials	5000 and 15,000 m	J-shaped, decreasing
	Proximity to roads	200 and 3000 m	J-shaped, decreasing

Table 4. Fuzzy set memberships and membership functions with control points used for MSW landfill site selection.

7.1.3.2. Olfactory and sonorous impacts

Concerning the olfactory and sonorous impacts factors, a simple linear distance decay function is appropriate for these criteria, in which a cost distance from the main roads increases, its suitability increases. To rescale the cost distance factor, a monotonically increasing linear fuzzy membership function was used. The first control point (a = 200 m) indicates the least suitable distance for siting a landfill while the second control point (b = 3000 m) and indicates the best fitted distance for siting a landfill (**Figure 3**).

7.1.4. Socio-economic factors

The socio-economic factors comprises three sub-factors namely proximity to dense population, distance from road and proximity to building materials.

7.1.5. Proximity to dense population

Proximity to the waste generation centers generate most of the waste quantity is a very significant factor because it defines the working costs for the landfill. The closer to the dense population settlements, the lower the operation cost will be. The population density map was standardized by sigmoid decreasing fuzzy function controlled by two points (c = 200 hab/km², d = 1000 hab/km²).

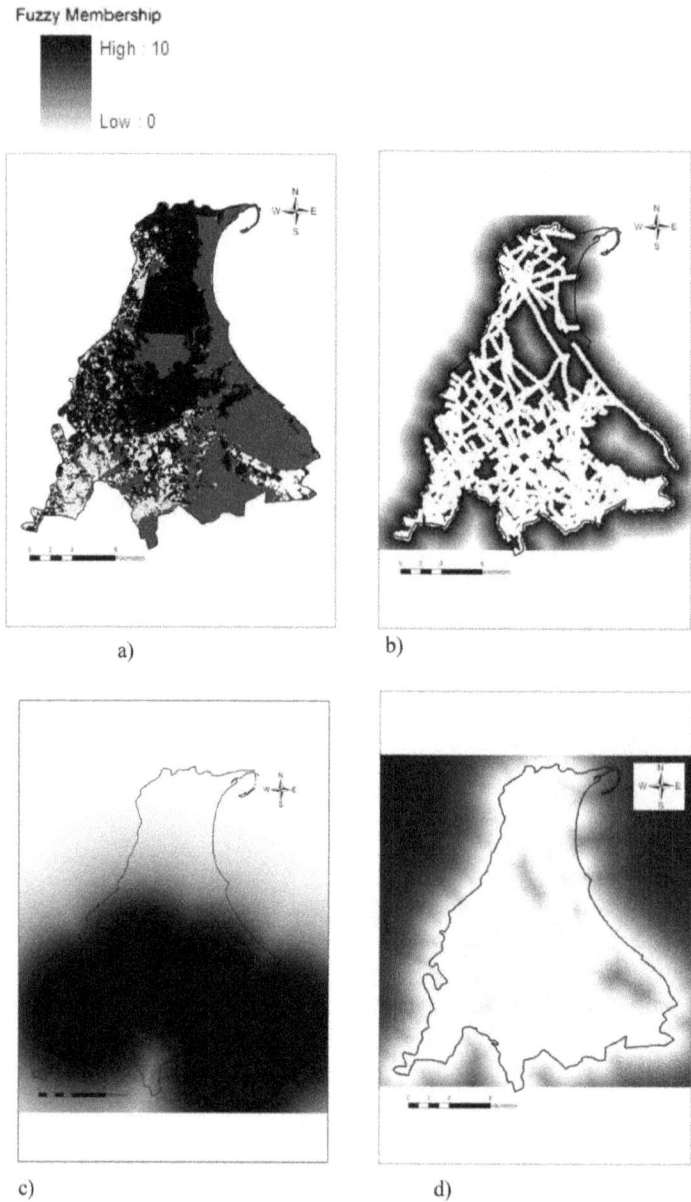

Figure 3. Examples of spatial evaluation maps of factors a) Land use, b) Olfactory and sonorous impacts, c) proximity to buildings materials, d) Distance from roads.

7.1.6. Proximity to roads

Proximity to roads considers the construction costs for building new road infrastructure between the settlements and potential landfill. A j-shaped decreasing fuzzy membership function was used for standardization controlled by two points (c = 200 m, d = 3000).

7.1.7. Proximity to building materials

Proximity to building materials is used for comparing the costs for building materials during landfill construction (impermeable soil for the bottom liner) and landfill operation (daily and final cover material). For sanitary landfills, such materials also minimize the propagation of various vectors (i.e., insects, rodents, birds and air contaminants) that may affect public health and well-being [4]. Again, a j-shaped decreasing function was used with two control points (c = 5000 m, d = 15,000).

The next step was implementation of the AHP to calculate the relative weights of the criteria. This step involved construction of comparison matrix where weights are determined through the pairwise comparison method. Pairwise comparison method was used only to assign weights and establish importance of environmental criteria using experience of experts and characteristics of the region (**Tables 5** and **6**).

The final stage is to calculate a CR to measure how consistent the judgments have been relative to large samples of purely random judgments. For the case study the CR was 0, indicating construction of a trustworthy matrix.

7.1.8. Scenario creation

WLC is displayed to compute the possible landfill areas for both of the environmental and socio-economic set of criteria, using the assigning weight to each of the criteria. Intermediate fitness maps were created for the environmental and socio-economic group of criteria, respectively. Final aggregation of the two intermediate suitability maps was implemented for three scenarios to demonstrate the importance of the weights associated with the environmental and

	Land use	Olfactory and sonorous impacts	Eigenvector	Weight
Land use	1	5	2.23	2.23/(2.23 + 0.45) = 0.83
Olfactory and sonorous impacts	1/5	1	0.45	0.45/(2.23 + 0.45) = 0.17
λ max=2, CI = 0.00, CR = 0.00 (consistency is acceptable).				

Table 5. Pair-wise comparison matrix for assessing the weights of environmental factors.

	Proximity to buildings materials	Proximity to dense population	Proximity to roads	Eigenvector	Weight
Proximity to buildings materials	1	1/5	1/3	0.44	0.11
Proximity to dense population	5	1	3	2.44	0.63
Proximity to roads	3	1/3	1	1	0.26
λ max=3.038, CI = 0.019, RI = 0.58, CR = 0.03 < <0.1 (consistency is acceptable).					

Table 6. Pair-wise comparison matrix for assessing the weights of socio-economic factors.

the socio-economic objectives. The WLC was used to create three final landfill suitability maps using different weights applied to the objectives. The scenario (a) allots a weight of 0.75 to the environmental and 0.25 to the socio-economic objective; for scenario (b) both objectives have the same weights and for scenario (c) weights of 0.25 and 0.75 are used for the environmental and the socio-economic objectives, respectively. It should be mentioned that we select the sustainable development scenario which assigned the equal weight to the environmental and socio-economical factors (0.5 for each factor). The final suitability map for the mentioned scenario is shown in **Figure 4**. Using an equal interval classification method, landfill suitability values of the Ariana region were classified into five groups: high suitability (8–10), suitable (8–6), moderate suitability (6–4) and low suitability (4–2) and very low suitable (2–0). This method divides the range of attribute values into equal-sized sub-ranges. This creates an easy to

Figure 4. Landfill suitability map.

understand legend and works best with continuously distributed data. Then, we grouped similar and adjoining pixels to keep sites having an area of greater than 28 ha, roughly 28 cells (100 × 100). The results indicate that 2.5%, of the study area has very low suitability, 3.9% has low suitability, 12.5% has moderate suitability, 0.5% has suitable and 5.4% has high suitability for a landfill site. The other 75.20% of the study area is not suitable for a landfill site. The results of the AHP and weighted linear combination methods are compatible with our field observations.

Two candidate sites (C1 and C2) were recommended for landfill siting because these regions were determined to be high suitability regions by the AHP and GIS techniques (**Figure 4**). These two candidate sites are away from the Sebkhat Ariana. C1 is located north of the Sebkhat Ariana around Raoued district. The wastes of Kalaat El Andalous and the surrounding vicinity can be collected at this site. The other candidate site (C2) is situated western of the Sebkhat Ariana, near the Sidi Thabet district, where it can collect waste from areas such as Ennahli and the villages between them.

8. Conclusions

Although it is very difficult and expensive to include geological, hydrological and hydrogeological, social, environmental and economical parameters, studies for selecting the sites for solid waste disposal should be performed for every city in Tunisia. To determine an appropriate landfill site, GIS is a very powerful tool that can provide a rapid assessment of the study area. The selection of suitable landfill sites is very decisive for Tunisia. Ariana region was selected as the study area because it is the fast growing and urban in greater Tunis. Initially, landfill site selection criteria were determined depending on the applicable international literature. Thirteen criteria were evaluated in the present study. The areas that were inappropriate for MSW landfill site were at first determined and covered. Thus, these areas were not considered. Each criterion was evaluated and converted into arithmetical values by AHP. The criteria maps were mapped by GIS using the calculated numerical values. Using the same interval classification method, the study area was classified into four groups of high, moderate, low and very low suitability, which covered 3.24, 7.55, 12.70 and 2.81% of the study area, respectively. The results of the analysis were compared with field studies, and two candidate landfill sites (C1 and C2) were selected from the high suitability regions. These sites are also close to highly populated settlements. Finally, it is recommended that the methodology adopted in this research to be developed through integrating the indigenous data which might lead to better site selection.

Author details

Abdelwaheb Aydi

Address all correspondence to: abdelwaheb_2000@yahoo.fr

Department of Earth Sciences, Faculty of Science of Bizerte, Carthage University, Bizerte, Tunisia

References

[1] Şener Ş, Sener E, Karagüzel R. Solid waste disposal site selection with GIS and AHP methodology: A case study in Senirkent–Uluborlu (Isparta) basin, Turkey. Environmental Monitoring and Assessment. 2011;**173**(1-4):533-554

[2] Chang N-B, Parvathinathan G, Breeden JB. Combining GIS with fuzzy multicriteria decision-making for landfill siting in a fast-growing urban region. Journal of Environmental Management. 2008;**87**(1):139-153

[3] Wang G et al. Landfill site selection using spatial information technologies and AHP: A case study in Beijing, China. Journal of Environmental Management. 2009;**90**(8):2414-2421

[4] Gorsevski PV et al. Integrating multi-criteria evaluation techniques with geographic information systems for landfill site selection: A case study using ordered weighted average. Waste Management. 2012;**32**(2):287-296

[5] Zamorano M et al. Evaluation of a municipal landfill site in southern Spain with GIS-aided methodology. Journal of Hazardous Materials. 2008;**160**(2-3):473-481

[6] Donevska KR et al. Regional non-hazardous landfill site selection by integrating fuzzy logic, AHP and geographic information systems. Environmental Earth Sciences. 2012;**67**(1):121-131

[7] Sharifi M et al. Integrating multi-criteria decision analysis for a GIS-based hazardous waste landfill sitting in Kurdistan Province, western Iran. Waste Management. 2009;**29**(10):2740-2758

[8] Khamehchiyan M, Nikoudel MR, Boroumandi M. Identification of hazardous waste landfill site: A case study from Zanjan province, Iran. Environmental Earth Sciences. 2011;**64**(7):1763-1776

[9] Nazari A, Salarirad MM, Bazzazi AA. Landfill site selection by decision-making tools based on fuzzy multi-attribute decision-making method. Environmental Earth Sciences. 2012;**65**(6):1631-1642

[10] Sahnoun H et al. GIS and multi-criteria analysis to select potential sites of agro-industrial complex. Environmental Earth Sciences. 2012;**66**(8):2477-2489

[11] Moeinaddini M et al. Siting MSW landfill using weighted linear combination and analytical hierarchy process (AHP) methodology in GIS environment (case study: Karaj). Waste Management. 2010;**30**(5):912-920

[12] Voogd H. Multicriteria Evaluation for Urban and Regional Planning. Vol. 207. London: Pion; 1983

[13] Mahini AS, Gholamalifard M. Siting MSW landfills with a weighted linear combination methodology in a GIS environment. International Journal of Environmental Science & Technology. 2006;**3**(4):435-445

[14] Saaty T. The Analytic Hierarchy Process. New York Google Scholar: McGraw-Hill; 1980

[15] Statistique, I.I.N.d.l., Données générales sur la population. données démographiques et sociales, 2011. < http://www.ins.nat.tn>

[16] Aouadhi H, B.S.M., Modes et Plans de Gestion des Déchets Ménagers dans le Grand Tunis. Institut Supérieur des Technologies de l'Environnement de l'Urbanisme & du Bâtiment, Projet de Fin d'étude, 2006

[17] Aydi A, Zairi M, Dhia HB. Minimization of environmental risk of landfill site using fuzzy logic, analytical hierarchy process, and weighted linear combination methodology in a geographic information system environment. Environmental Earth Sciences. 2013;**68**(5):1375-1389

[18] Saaty TL. A scaling method for priorities in hierarchical structures. Journal of Mathematical Psychology. 1977;**15**(3):234-281

[19] Eastman JR, Kyem PA, Toledano J. A procedure for multi-objective decision making in GIS under conditions of conflicting objectives. In: Proceedings of the Fourth European Conference on Geographic Information Systems. 1993

[20] Eastman JR. IDRISI 32 release 2. Guide to GIS and Image Processing, 2001. **2**:p. 01610-1477

www.ingramcontent.com/pod-product-compliance
Lightning Source LLC
Chambersburg PA
CBHW081236190326
41458CB00016B/5803